BACKSTAIRS
BILLY

BACKSTAIRS
BILLY

The Life of
WILLIAM TALLON
the Queen Mother's Most Devoted Servant

Tom Quinn

The Robson Press

First published in Great Britain in 2015 by
The Robson Press (an imprint of Biteback Publishing Ltd)
Westminster Tower
3 Albert Embankment
London SE1 7SP

ISBN 978-1-84954-780-2

10 9 8 7 6 5 4 3 2 1

A CIP catalogue record for this book is available from the British Library.

Set in Adobe Caslon Pro

Printed and bound in Great Britain by
CPI Group (UK) Ltd, Croydon CR0 4YY

MIX
Paper from
responsible sources
FSC
www.fsc.org
FSC® C020471

Contents

Introduction

AT THE TIME of his death in 2007, William John Stephenson Tallon, or 'Backstairs Billy' as he was known, was familiar to a relatively small circle that included the members of the royal family, but especially Prince Charles and Lord Snowdon, and a long list of former homosexual lovers, many of whom had also been in royal service. Outside that circle Billy was not at that time widely known, but in the years since his death a picture has emerged of a man whose life was extraordinary by any standards.

It was extraordinary because Tallon was always an unlikely candidate to be part of the intimate royal circle.

William Tallon spent more than half a century working for the royal family at Buckingham Palace and Clarence House. Nominally, he was a servant; in reality, he was a uniquely trusted friend and confidant to the Queen Mother. Other friends and advisers came and went but Billy was a man the Queen Mother could never quite do without. The history of their remarkable relationship is the subject of this book.

Though intensely loyal, Billy was also a dangerous risk taker; though charming he could also be vicious; though considerate and amusing he could also be ruthless and predatory.

This is the story of a curiously contradictory man and it is a story that has never before been told. For the first time since Billy's death, many of those who knew him have agreed to talk about Billy and their memories add up to a picture of a complex man who, with none of the usual qualifications of birth and privilege, became a central figure in one of the world's most admired institutions.

I met William Tallon a number of times during the last years of his life. I met some of his friends and a number of his former colleagues. Most of his friends were people he met socially; his few enemies tended to be those with whom he had worked.

There is no doubt that if William Tallon took to someone he was wonderfully good company – he was funny, talkative and very witty. And he loved gossip. He could make a story come to life as no one else could. He could also be very kind. But occasionally he would take against someone and then he could be very unkind indeed.

He was a creature of extremes: he was immensely loyal to his friends, but very spiteful to his enemies. For much of his life he was driven by two demons: a powerful sex drive and an intense, almost pathological love for the Queen Mother.

I've spoken to and corresponded with more of Billy's enemies and former colleagues than his friends. His friends understandably remember only the witty storyteller, the generous host, the performer, so their memories tend to cast a rosy glow. Billy's colleagues and subordinates, not all of whom disliked him, add the shadows and most of the deeper complexities, and so their memories, perhaps inevitably, make up a greater part of this book.

One difficulty with a book such as this – one that portrays someone only very recently dead – is that the subject's contemporaries are wary of upsetting others still alive. But, even allowing for that, I was still surprised at quite how many of those who talked to me were willing to help only if they were not identified. Some are still working in service and feared they would be dismissed if they were quoted in anything controversial. Others felt their memories were still too raw to be acknowledged openly. For good or ill, I agreed to these requests for anonymity, or for a change of name, for without them this book could not have been written.

As the years go by, memories of this fascinating – some would say wholly remarkable – character will inevitably fade, especially as he was someone whose life was not, as it were, part of official record. He was not in any real sense a public figure; yet he was often the subject of public, especially media, speculation. He cannot, however, be described as an entirely private figure either.

William Tallon was in truth that rarest of all rare creatures, a very ordinary person who carved out an extraordinary role for himself in one of the world's most secretive institutions: the British royal family. On the face of it, he was the last person one would have expected to reach a position of influence among the royals. He had very little formal education and came from a working-class background, yet, relying entirely on personality and force of character, he became, in many ways, one of the most significant characters in a world where education and social class meant everything.

But if it is hard to write about a royal servant, it is even more difficult to write about a member of the royal family.

The sensitivities involved in any discussion of the Queen Mother and other members of the royal family are legion. Any and every book published about the Windsors is either derided as sycophantic or attacked for denigrating the members of one of our most cherished institutions.

The newspapers' usual technique is to track down an elderly, distant relative of the royal family who then denounces the book as a tissue of lies and insults. This kind of automatic reaction is largely based on a desire to preserve an image of the royal family as symbols rather than real people. Critics of books about the royals would have us believe that members of the royal family do not have flesh-and-blood lives with faults and foibles like the rest of us. The case is particularly acute with the Queen Mother, who was by any standards a remarkable and in many ways admirable woman. But are we really to believe she never lost her temper, never became confused or embarrassed, never drank a little too much? And we are forced to ask the question: does it really damage the Queen Mother's reputation to report that she liked jokes and gossip, that she enjoyed dancing and games and horseplay? Backstairs Billy once said that the great thing about the Queen Mother was that she liked to have fun and didn't care who knew it and in this, as in many other ways, he was almost certainly right.

TWO HUNDRED GUESTS, including HM the Queen's cousin Lord Snowdon and actors Patricia Routledge and Sir Derek Jacobi, gathered at the Queen's Chapel in St James's Palace on a cold winter's day in 2007. Hundreds more had applied for tickets for a most unusual funeral service.

A casual observer might have assumed some great dignitary had passed on.

In fact the service was for a working-class boy born above a hardware shop in a run-down town in Co. Durham during the Great Depression; a boy who grew to become one of the late Queen Mother's most trusted aides.

One of the difficulties of writing about Billy was that he was himself naturally inclined to secrecy and this tendency was intensified by a lifetime's devotion to a job where discretion, loyalty and secrecy were vital. But Billy also liked to embellish and to some extent he was a master of evasion and fantasy. Sometimes his exaggerations were entirely unnecessary. If he *was* so very close to the Queen Mother, why was he at pains to over-state the case?

It is difficult to separate truth from fiction in many areas of his life because all those who have written about him – including friends and journalists – have had an agenda according to whether they liked or loathed him. Some say, for example, that Billy was the only male member of staff permitted to enter the Queen Mother's bedroom without knocking. Others say this is nonsense and that although he carried the breakfast tray to her room he always left it outside for her personal maid to carry in. Some insist that Billy was so manipulative that the Queen Mother was almost afraid of him. Others insist this is nonsense and that the Queen Mother delighted in keeping her sometimes-wayward page in check. In these and in so many other ways there is something mysterious about Billy and his life. He and others embellished almost everything to do with his role in the royal household. It was as if during his long life in service he became a character in a play, a play directed largely by himself.

Chapter One

Joining the royals

MILLIONS OF PEOPLE around the world are fascinated by the British royal family. The children of Her Majesty the Queen may have had messy divorces and given embarrassing interviews to the press at various times, but the Queen herself famously never complains and never explains.

On royal tours and the endless series of visits and events that make up the royal calendar, we watch as the royal presence conjures a magical world of ritual through the State Opening of Parliament, Trooping the Colour, Changing of the Guard, not to mention processions down the Mall with various foreign heads of state.

The Queen is a familiar figure, yet she seems both well known and, at the same time, profoundly unknowable. There is no chink in her armour; no hint at a genuinely private life behind the facade.

Until her death in 2002, there was only one figure who rivalled the Queen in terms of the world's interest and the nation's affection, and that was her mother. Like her daughter, Elizabeth the Queen Mother never gave interviews; never explained, never complained. She seemed to float – cynics would say on a tide of gin – above criticism.

But, unlike her daughter, the Queen Mother *was* occasionally indiscreet and frequently off-message. This was perhaps because she had married rather than been born into the royal family. Indeed, when the prospect first appeared on the horizon, she had been horrified at the idea of being a member of the royal family for precisely the reason that she knew her life would never be normal again.

THE BOWES-LYON FAMILY were certainly aristocratic, but when Elizabeth Bowes-Lyon married Albert, Duke of York in 1923, the more conservative elements of the British establishment were aghast that the young prince had not been persuaded to marry a foreign princess. Elizabeth's father, it is true, was the Earl of Strathmore and Kinghorne, but, despite this, it was thought by some that a minor German princess might have been preferable to a mere aristocrat. From the perspective of the early twenty-first century such things may seem ridiculous, but in the early part of the twentieth century they were considered of the first importance.

However, there was less to worry about than might at first appear. As the more conservative members of the royal family's advisers pointed out, Elizabeth Bowes-Lyon's young husband Albert, the second son of King George V and Queen Mary, was never going to become king. In fact, it was only the shocking abdication of her husband's brother in 1936 that led to a change in Elizabeth's fortunes that no one could have predicted. She might otherwise have lived out her life in wealth and relative obscurity, able to do and say more or less as she pleased.

But, for all the complaints about a lack of royal blood, Elizabeth had no doubts about her position. She grew up in the decade before the Great War when the British aristocracy simply assumed that their vast landed fortunes – untaxed and unencumbered by death duties – would last forever. The taste for the high life that those fortunes created never left Elizabeth Bowes-Lyon, who, to the end of her life, spent money as if it really did grow on trees.

Too polite to speculate about royal extravagance during her lifetime, the public did begin to speculate – and with a vengeance – once the Queen Mother died.

Despite the criticisms, however, it must have been difficult for Elizabeth to imagine a world where servants did not provide every possible creature comfort, where tradesmen did not deliver the finest food and wine at the back door and where, having made their deliveries, they were not paid by a housekeeper or butler so that the head of the family need never be bothered by anything so sordid as money.

Elizabeth's lifestyle was fundamentally the same in 2000 as it had been in 1930. It reflected precisely an earlier era when the aristocracy and the royal family could simply do as they pleased and the taxpayer must uncomplainingly foot the bill.

Some idea of the world in which Elizabeth grew up can be gleaned from the fact that only a few decades before her birth, an official in the Government tax office (as it then was) pointed out that it was rather undignified for the royal family to pay any tax at all. They *had* paid tax without complaint for as long as anyone could remember, but quietly, and without a word of dissent from Parliament or the press, the royal family was immediately made exempt from all income tax – a situation that remained unchanged until the 1990s.

The fact is that the Queen Mother famously spent money as she pleased and was hugely in debt at the time of her death. According to various newspaper reports, which admittedly it is difficult to verify, she owed her bankers, Coutts, more than £7 million and the joke in Clarence House, her home for more than fifty years, was that nobody could be found who had the courage to tell her that the money would have to be paid back. Again unconfirmed reports suggest that the Queen Mother's daughter Queen Elizabeth, in order to avoid the inevitable scandal, quietly repaid the huge debt.

Living a life that was rather like a fairy-tale fantasy was the only life Elizabeth ever knew and it was this fairy-tale life that was to draw William Tallon into royal service for more than five decades. As he also would have no doubt been aware, not telling the royals embarrassing truths has a long history.

When the Labouchere Amendment was passed in England in 1881 (replacing the earlier crime of buggery) all homosexual acts between men became known, for the purposes of the law, as 'gross indecency'. At the time it was thought wise to include a clause banning female homosexuality also, but when it was realised that this clause would have to be seen by Queen Victoria when she signed the Bill into law, Parliament reacted with horror. Someone would actually have to explain to Her Majesty what lesbianism involved. This was unthinkable. The clause was hastily removed and female homosexuality was never made illegal as a result.

The terror of bringing bad or awkward and embarrassing news to the royals continued more or less unchanged until the death of Diana, Princess of Wales. Her passion for complaining and explaining to the press, and to anyone else who would listen, exposed the royal family to unprecedented criticism and even the Queen temporarily lost some of her allure. Yet even at this difficult time – a time when it is generally agreed the monarchy came close to collapse – the Queen Mother sailed through relatively unscathed.

The cracks really only appeared after she had died because memories of royal criticism following Diana's death were fresh in people's minds. It was permissible to criticise where abuses were rampant because a new precedent had been set. When the royal family gathered in black at the gates of Buckingham Palace to watch Diana's funeral cortege, many claimed, perhaps unfairly, that they were there not because they wanted to be but because they wanted to head off the risk of a huge public backlash.

Surprise at the state of the Queen Mother's finances led inevitably to speculation about her entourage. To the end of her life, she is rumoured to have employed around sixty personal attendants at any one time. This seemed an almost medieval extravagance to some commentators and the low pay that these servants – for that is what they were – often received only increased their indignation.

As one newspaper columnist put it, average pay below stairs in the royal household was sometimes on a par with that of a road sweeper, and yet servants were routinely expected to work extraordinarily long hours.

*S*ERVANTS HAVE ALWAYS been the one weak spot in the royal defences. They are relatively badly paid so they are always a risk as the newspapers are inevitably keen to pay for stories about Britain's most secretive and famous family.

The late Princess of Wales's butler Paul Burrell is a good example. His book about life as a servant with the royals caused a scandal, not because he revealed embarrassing secrets but because he claimed an intimacy with Diana that many questioned.

Back in the 1940s Marion Crawford – nanny to Princess

Elizabeth and her sister Margaret – had also famously written a book about her experiences. This shone a relatively innocuous light on the hidden world of the royals but despite the fact that the book gave very little away and simply served, as it were, to polish the reputations of the royals, poor Nanny Crawford was never forgiven and was never again contacted by the children she had cherished through their early years.

Despite their so-called revelations, Marion Crawford and Paul Burrell were benign interpreters of life behind the royal facade. Far more dangerous, potentially, was the man who became the most famous ex-royal servant of all: Backstairs Billy.

Billy never wrote a book, although at the time of his death his friends were convinced he was at work on his memoirs. But even without written evidence from Billy himself, his love–hate relationship with the royals can be pieced together from a wide range of sources, but especially former fellow servants, as well as friends and lovers.

*A*NYONE WHO HAS ever watched any public event that involved the Queen Mother at its centre will have noticed a distinguished-looking man always in close attendance, but lagging behind the Queen Mother at a discreet distance. This was William Tallon, or Backstairs Billy.

He always looked the same, hardly seeming to age as the years passed and almost always in charge of the corgis or helping collect spontaneous gifts from the public. With his long, brushed-back hair which apparently remained dark well into middle age, his elegant, perfectly worn morning suit and medals, Tallon seemed to embody all that we think we know about the royals' upper-class attendants.

In fact Billy always looked far too grand, too much the commanding presence, to be described as a servant; his regal air extended to smiling and waving to the crowd, even, on occasion, stopping to engage in small talk, as if he really were a member of the royal family.

Indeed, Billy was thought by many unsuspecting members of the public to be a relative or personal friend of the Queen Mother. Certainly he was seen as coming from a similar social stratum.

Most people thought Billy was at the very least a public-school-educated equerry much like the other equerries in the royal household, who were and are still largely drawn from the middle and upper classes. But Billy was nothing of the kind. As we have seen, he was a shopkeeper's son from the north of England. Yet, despite his humble origins, he was to beat the equerries at their own game.

Chapter Two

Working for the firm

T HE ROYAL FAMILY'S advisers are usually, though not always, drawn from what used to be called 'the top drawer'. They are often old Etonians or old Harrovians who have formerly been officers in the 'best' regiments – typically the Household Cavalry.

No one ever seems to notice that the royals vary rarely employ what we might describe as ordinary people in these roles. The public schools supply the advisers while state schools provide the staff for jobs in the kitchens, the gardens and the stables; ordinary mortals work as maids and cleaners, hall boys, junior footmen and butlers. You might be forgiven, while in the royal household, for thinking you were in a medieval court of some kind. When it comes to working for the royals, the lines of social demarcation are pretty strict.

Backstairs Billy was different. He was rather like a private in the army who becomes a field marshal. Despite his origins, he rose to become unusually powerful in the royal household. Formally, his job defined him as not from the top drawer. Yet in his role as both servant and intimate adviser he blurred those strict lines of demarcation.

Much has been said about the veracity of Billy's claims concerning his closeness to the Queen Mother, and the power he claimed to have over her, but whatever his pretentions, it is highly likely that the Queen Mother's affection for Billy was largely a result of genuine sympathy and trust, but also her way of teasing the well-born advisers. Certainly Billy seems to have been disliked by the rather grand advisers who, then and now, inhabit the royal corridors above stairs. In Billy's day, they simply could not understand why the Queen Mother seemed so fond of what they may have seen as a 'rather common' man.

The truth is almost certainly that the Queen Mother's affection for Billy was genuine. She liked Billy because he was amusing, devoted and discreet in those areas that mattered to her. But she never thought of him in the way she thought of her advisers. She had been born at a time when such distinctions were automatic and if someone from the lower ranks happened to be given particular notice of favour this was always combined with a sense that that favour could be withdrawn at any time. One's friends, on the other hand, were one's friends precisely because they came from the same social stratum.

Remarkably, Billy's relationship with the Queen Mother echoes Queen Victoria's relationship with her gillie John Brown. Although a servant, Brown was treated with enormous respect and affection by the Queen. It has been said that Victoria's passion for all things Scottish was really a reflection of her passion for Brown. Certainly, until his death in 1883 Queen Victoria spent every moment when she was at Balmoral with a man who, by all accounts, treated her with a shocking disregard for convention. He made jokes and teased her at one moment and spoke sharply the next.

Despite, or perhaps because of, this over-familiarity, Brown was adored by Victoria, so far as we can tell from reports made at the time. But she would never have thought of Brown as a friend outside the confines of her Scottish holidays. If anyone doubts Victoria's genuine affection for Brown, however, we need only remind ourselves that in her instructions for what should happen after her death she insisted – to the scandalised outrage of her advisers – that Brown's photograph, rather than that of her late husband Prince Albert, should be buried with her. There is also some evidence, including the deathbed confession of a Presbyterian minister, that Victoria actually married Brown in a secret ceremony towards the end of the gillie's life.

Nothing quite like this happened with Backstairs Billy but

the story of his rise and fall provides a fascinating insight into a world where the power of personality may sometimes outweigh the power of convention.

⧼⧽

𝐵ACKSTAIRS BILLY WAS a complex man who, in truth, both loved and occasionally loathed the royals; he was addicted to being part of their glamorous world and he revelled in the theatre that life as a royal servant provided. Billy was somehow vulnerable and yet also supremely manipulative; he was at times an immensely serious man and at others obsessed with trivia and the outward display of his own importance. But to the last he loved, perhaps more than anything, what might best be called the high camp of royal service.

I knew Billy only when his life had begun to spiral downwards. In his small flat in Kennington, south London, he seemed a forlorn figure, but perhaps no more so than many men without family, who, finding themselves retired from a job they once loved, feel that life is empty and largely meaningless.

But there was always an edge to Billy's tone when he talked about the royal family in general and the Queen Mother in particular. Many of those who knew him towards the end of his life have argued that his love for the Queen Mother refused to admit the least hint of criticism of her, but this seems in many ways to be an attempt to protect him from the bitterness of his own decline.

Indirectly and by implication he was in fact occasionally critical of her. He felt she should perhaps have done more to protect him from what he called the 'royal wolves'.

Several of his friends knew that he would like to be remembered only as a loyal servant and they assumed that his bitter attacks on those he felt had ousted him from the royal household were simply the result of old age and illness and not of real feeling. This seems to me to be a misreading for the sake of posthumous reputation. Billy did feel let down at the end of his life. He felt he had been harshly treated, but his unhappiness was compounded by the knowledge that to some extent he had brought disaster upon himself; he had made enemies where he should have made friends and he had been blind to the realities of his position. In fact, Billy's life might be seen as an almost perfect exemplar of the ancient warning that hubris leads inevitably to nemesis.

Chapter Three

Northern lights

IRTLEY IS A small town centred on the now-vanished Durham coalfield and a few miles south of Gateshead, the town on the south bank of the River Tyne with Newcastle a little to the north. Northumberland and Durham are economically depressed areas with high levels of social deprivation, high unemployment and, for the majority of ordinary people, few prospects. In the 1930s it was far worse.

The biggest employers today are the Royal Ordnance Factory and the Japanese engineering firm Komatsu, who make high-tech mining equipment. When William John Stephenson Tallon was born here at home on 12 November 1935, the town's Victorian terraced houses and municipal buildings would have been black with the soot of thousands of domestic coal fires, the pollution-filled air alive with talk of what went on in the mines and factories. Billy was born above his father's hardware shop at 27 Durham Road and, despite high levels of infant mortality in solidly working-class districts such as this, Billy was a robust, lively baby – 'a strong 'un' – who was hardly ever ill.

Birtley was a dark, forbidding place and people rarely risked showing their neighbours they aspired to anything out of the ordinary. In this respect and others, the town was very much like Hunslet, described in Richard Hoggart's famous book *The Uses of Literacy* on working-class life in the north of England. Birtley was a place where, as Hoggart memorably puts it, the local and the personal counted for everything. Abstract discussions about life in general, aspirations to get on, any kind of ambition beyond the local were all frowned upon and children were expected to go into the local factories just as their fathers and grandfathers had done. Girls could expect to marry in their late teens or early twenties, have children and run a home on what was usually a pitifully small income.

Alfred Gill, who was born in Birtley in 1940, recalled the narrowness of this industrial world:

> I don't recall anyone really getting away because there was a feeling

you shouldn't try to be better than your dad, your friends and their dads. It was a pride thing that you would do as your dad had done. I only heard of one boy who passed his eleven plus and went to grammar school and I think he became a bit of an outcast, or at least he was isolated in a way.

The idea of going to London even for a visit was like the idea of going to the moon. A charabanc to the seaside once a year was about the best we could hope for!

Another near contemporary of Billy's, who was born a few years later and just a few streets from his birthplace, recalled, 'You didn't expect much out of life in Birtley, but it was the same across much of the old industrial north east. Life revolved around the pub, the pit and the factory gates.'

But if life really did match the cliché of the north before the Second World War – a mix of pub, pit, whippets and ferrets – it was at least a close-knit community where families had often lived side by side for several generations. And there was always work in the mines and factories as well as trips to the seaside and even occasionally to the early cinema.

But by all accounts Billy's parents felt – like most shopkeepers at the time – that they were very slightly a cut above the rest. They didn't work in the mines or the factories and though they only sold hardware they felt they were business people with a degree of financial independence. It was true that, like all shopkeepers of the time in northern industrial towns, they had to sell goods 'on tick' – if they hadn't business would have soon dried up – but as

Alfred Gill recalled, 'shopkeepers definitely had more money than the rest of us and they looked down slightly on their customers. They felt that they were lower middle class if you like, rather than obviously working class.'

This sense of slight otherness would have been very similar to that felt by the late Margaret Thatcher – another shopkeeper's child from the provinces. It was a vague sense of superiority but one tinged with uncertainty about one's place in society. Margaret Thatcher's father compensated by becoming an ardent Tory; it was his way of nailing his colours to the middle-class mast. But for Margaret Thatcher and Billy Tallon this early social uncertainty led them to want to escape into a different world; a world that represented everything their home towns could not give them.

BIRTLEY OWED ITS origins to the demand for coal to fuel the Industrial Revolution. Few of the houses, factories and municipal buildings in the town had been built earlier than 1850 when the main Anglican church was constructed. Rows of dingy back-to-back terraced houses stretched in every direction.

The whole family, Billy's parents, grandparents and his sister Jennie, lived above the shop, but conditions at home were far better than those for many of the town's children who lived in tiny damp houses with outside lavatories and tin baths hanging on shed walls. These vermin-infested terraces were largely demolished during the 1960s and 1970s, but in the 1930s they were the only houses available.

So far as anyone can tell, the Tallons had lived in the area since at least the mid-nineteenth century, but it is almost certain the family originally came from Cornwall or Ireland. Certainly the name 'Tallon' is of Celtic origin.

Billy's paternal grandparents arrived as part of a wave of migration from the countryside to the north east of England and other mining and industrial centres during the boom years of the mid-nineteenth century when Durham and Yorkshire pits provided a seemingly endless supply of the cheap, high-quality coal that helped make Britain the manufacturing hub of the world.

Somehow, Billy's grandparents saved enough money during the final decades of the 1800s to buy the shop and the rooms above. They chose to sell hardware – everyday stuff that people would always need to buy and replace regularly: pots and pans, nails, brooms, dustbins, tools, lamps and even bicycles.

Billy rarely talked about his early days but he once confided to a friend:

> Although I left Birtley when I was just one and therefore don't remember a thing about it, it was something we talked about. We had been able to move which most of the other people in the town would never have contemplated, so I think I did feel different. Shopkeepers were always a slight oddity in any town and it was no different when we moved because we had another shop. But I always reminded myself in later years that Fortnum & Mason was started by two footmen who worked in St James's Palace. Shopkeepers had an independent spirit and I think that background gave me a lifelong belief that I was destined for higher things.

This sense of being different was even reflected in the name the Tallons gave their son. He was given the same name as his father – William – but his extra middle name 'Stephenson' was his mother Mabel's maiden name and she believed it was important that her son should have this name because she believed – probably correctly – that she was distantly related to the north-east's most famous son: the George Stephenson who built the first public railway in 1830. Railway Stephenson was born just thirty miles from Birtley in the village of Wylam on the banks of the River Tyne. Mabel, unlike William Senior, was a local girl and proud of it.

Adding this name to their son's other names suggested they had high hopes for him, but it also reveals his mother's powerful influence in the family. Billy revered his mother and though he loved his amiable father it was Mabel who dominated his early years and gave him a vague yearning for a more glamorous life. Mabel was always at pains to remind Billy that his family was well connected; they were not working class, they were middle class and she had a taste for the finer things that William undoubtedly inherited.

'She loved coloured glass and knick-knacks,' he recalled years later. 'And china. She had a very good eye.'

John Robson, who lived in Birtley during the 1940s, remembered that the shopkeepers' sense that they were different made them unpopular in some quarters:

> The shopkeepers didn't have to get their hands dirty. This was a rock-solid socialist area and during the 1930s and 1940s many even turned

to the Communist Party. Communists hated the shopkeepers because they saw them as mini-capitalists exploiting the poor almost as much as the factory and mine owners. It was a bit unfair because some shopkeepers had just had a bit of luck or spent less on drink and managed to save up. But it was no better if their grandfather had been a miner and they'd bettered themselves. Trying to get on was seen often as a sort of class betrayal.

Billy's mother would have risen above these concerns. Neighbours and friends remember her as 'a nice woman but a bit aloof'. She was a serious woman who gave customers in the hardware shop credit but disliked doing it. She would complain that if people managed their money better and stayed out of the pub they would not need her to provide credit all the time. This undiplomatic attitude created a certain distance between the Tallons and the people among whom they lived. As one neighbour put it:

> People in those days were desperate not to be looked down on, but Mabel made a point of looking down on you or at least appearing to. She was polite enough to your face but she had a hard streak. I always thought her perm said it all – her hair was never a fraction out of place. Very severe.

The golden rule among the factory workers and the miners was that people should not 'get above themselves', but Mabel was determined to be seen as a cut above the rest.

By the time Billy was born, the boom years in the north-east were over. The steady decline that was to lead to the closure of every mine in Durham during the 1970s and 1980s had begun. Birtley, like much of the north-east, was in the grip of the worst recession in history.

Like many families the Tallons were badly hit. With layoffs and falling demand for the industrial products of the town, the hardware business virtually collapsed. Try as the family did to scrimp and save to keep the business afloat until better times came along, it was impossible. In 1937 the business failed and the family sold up and moved south to Coventry where there was more work and therefore better prospects.

Details of Billy's early life are hard to come by but according to Coventry records and those whose recollections of him go back to childhood it seems that the family used the money from the sale of the shop in Birtley to buy the house in Coundon, a suburb of Coventry, and they worked only sporadically thereafter. It seems they had enough money – but only just.

Despite being devoted to their son, Billy's parents seem to have made no attempt to get him into an especially good school and they were quite happy to allow him to leave at the first opportunity.

Billy rarely talked about his parents to his colleagues in later life, but this is not unusual when someone moves from one social stratum to another. There is almost always a degree of embarrassment, or at least compartmentalisation. The playwright Alan Bennett famously said that when he went to Oxford from his Leeds grammar school he quickly found his parents embarrassing and tried to avoid letting them come to see him in Oxford.

Something similar seems to have happened to Billy, but like Bennett he loved his parents and returned regularly to the house in Coundon to see them. In later years as his royal responsibilities grew his visits became less frequent, but he never entirely forgot his origins or the people he had known as a child.

Coventry contemporaries were to become proud of Billy's royal connection and he did mix with them whenever he returned to see his parents. He also invited one or two close friends to visit him if they happened to be in London. In turn, Billy was justifiably proud that he was able to offer guided tours of Clarence House. But, when his mother Mabel finally died in the 1970s he cut his ties with Coventry and it seems he never again visited the city.

When the Tallons arrived in Coundon, the terraced house in which they settled in Norman Place Road was by no means the worst in the town. In fact, Coundon was considered one of the better districts. It had only recently lost its status as a village – Coventry's house-building boom swamped the old village in the years leading up to Billy's birth but it was still recognised by the older residents as having a distinct difference from Coventry. Some residents welcomed the fact that it would now be part of a bigger town; others lamented the loss of its independence.

Billy, a year old when the family moved, was to spend the rest of his childhood in Coundon, but he never really regarded it as home. He always felt on the edge of things, an outsider. This was undoubtedly partly due to the growing realisation that he was homosexual, but far more to attitudes he had clearly learned from his mother and during his long years in royal service he would always groan if anyone asked him about his childhood. In fact, it eventually became almost a no-go area for conversation and fellow servants were always careful to avoid the subject. Peter Livesey, who worked in the royal kitchens during the 1970s and 1980s, remembered that Billy made a point of behaving in an aloof manner until he got to know you, but even then his conversation was always rooted in the present.

> However much he liked you, he hated it if you were 'cheeky', which meant asking any questions about his past – I mean before he joined the royals. He really wanted people to think that he was well born. It wasn't exactly that he was ashamed of his origins or that he told lies about the past but he had a reluctance to talk about a life he had clearly been desperate to escape.

Billy vanishes for a while after the move from Birtley to Coventry apart from occasional glimpses of a lively child who ran about the streets but was curiously fastidious. Friends recall a boy who hated to get his clothes dirty and disliked football, which made him very much the odd man out. He had a reputation for being a bit of a sissy but this was combined with an inner toughness. He may not have been much good in a scrap but he was a sarcastic and quick-witted boy who was good at making the bullies feel foolish. One contemporary remembered that though Billy wasn't sporty and hated to get into fights, he already had a 'savage tongue'. It was something he had inherited from his mother, who was well known for her waspish put-downs and for the speed and fearlessness with which she delivered them. No one ever complained in the Tallons' shop or was rude to her face because she could turn in a second. 'One minute she was all smiles then next she'd torn your character to shreds with a pointed one-liner,' recalled one of Billy's early friends.

Once, when a boy said something rude about Billy's mother he was livid and in a split second he turned to the boy – who had a reputation for fighting – and spat out, 'I don't know that your mother is any better – all fur coat and no knickers, I've heard!'

The next we hear of Billy is when he went, aged eleven, to the local school, Barker's Butts.

The school had come into existence, in the form in which Billy knew it, following the Education Act of 1944. This set up a tripartite system, with grammar schools taking the top ten to fifteen per cent of each age group (these were the elite), technical schools taking those who were deemed intelligent but of a more practical bent, and finally secondary moderns, notoriously bad schools that were effectively dumping grounds for those deemed good for little more than factory work, driving buses or sweeping the streets.

Billy failed his eleven plus and had no choice but to attend a school that had low expectations for its pupils and could attract only those teachers who could not get jobs elsewhere. He was immensely intelligent, as his later career was to show, but, like so many boys condemned to a dreary future by the old tripartite system, he was rejected by a system that gave you one chance and one chance only at age eleven.

Billy began to think for himself in his mid-teens but by then it was too late – the end of his school days was already looming. He may have collected beautiful china and pictures later in life but he rarely read for pleasure and had no interest in books generally – both legacies of those early uninspiring years.

But even Billy was surprised that, unlike other aspiring Coventry parents, Mabel and William Sr had not tried harder to get him through the eleven plus and into grammar school.

'I think they were just tired by then,' he recalled. 'And they themselves were not academic or ambitious for me in any particular way. I don't think they really understood the system either; the implications, I mean, of failure at age eleven.'

But, whatever his parents' level of interest, there is no doubt that Barker's Butts was what today would be described as a 'sink school'. Although many ex-pupils remember enjoying their time there, none made any claim for it as a place that taught you to have high aspirations. Peter McGrath attended in the 1950s. He recalled:

> Well, when you are in your early teens you're barely aware what sort of school you're attending, especially if you come from a working-class background. You just go where you are sent and Barker's Butts had some good teachers, or at least teachers who cared about us – and we had a great football team!

The problem was that Barker's Butts worked on the principle that the children in its care needed only a very basic education – a smattering of geography and history and arithmetic, a bit of reading and English grammar, but no French or Latin, no physics or biology. Pupils were being made ready for lives as factory workers and bus drivers, shop workers and dustbin men. The only compensation was that daily life among one's friends made up for some of what the school lacked. Billy later insisted that though the school offered little, he was not particularly unhappy.

With little academic ambition for its pupils, many of whom were sent out on projects to count the number of cars passing along the street or given other inane tasks just to keep them occupied, Barker's Butts was a drab environment for a boy with ideas above his station.

The school that Billy knew was demolished in the 1960s as part of a local education authority re-organisation. Architecturally it was typical of early twentieth-century board schools – red brick with tall windows and a vaguely Queen Anne appearance. Unlike many board schools, which were and are rather elegant, Barker's Butts was a long, low building. Other pupils remember the school with a mixture of resignation and downright hostility. Reg Cotter, who was two years ahead of Billy, recalled, 'We knew we'd failed from the age of eleven.'

The lucky few who avoided Barker's Butts went on to grammar school, which meant a professional job and maybe even university in Leeds or Birmingham. Barker's Butts was what people called the factory kids' school because without a miracle – and there were few enough of those at the time in Coventry – the factory was the chief employer of ex-pupils. A number of boys recalled that the only relief from the sense that you had failed was sport.

The football club – rugby was for the grammar school boys – made life bearable for those who were good at sport. But this only left Billy on the side-lines both literally and metaphorically.

But if the school lacked the polish of the local grammar school, the city of Coventry wasn't much better.

Coventry in the late 1930s was one of the best-preserved medieval cities in Europe, but when Billy was seven it was largely destroyed by the Luftwaffe in a series of night-time air raids that set light easily to the ancient dried timbers of the city's houses.

Billy may well have just about remembered the city before the terrible bombing that laid waste to it.

> It had been a beautiful, largely unspoiled and still recognisably medieval city filled with narrow lanes and picturesque fifteenth- and sixteenth-century timber-framed buildings. But we took it for granted and, in fact, many people, especially on the council, actually hated it. They thought it was old and worn out, a load of rubbish, an embarrassment.

But if the city centre had survived the bombs it would have been destroyed anyway in the 1960s when much of what did survive the war was destroyed by the planning department of the council. Billy once said, 'I might have gone back if Coventry hadn't been turned into one of the ugliest places in Europe. After the 1960s it was ghastly for anyone who loved beautiful things. A real shock.'

This was another reason Billy hardly ever returned in later life to the city of his early years. 'Coventry is a terrible place,' he would say. 'It was beautiful if boring when I lived there as a boy but the planners finished what the Luftwaffe began and now no sane person would spend any more time there than he or she absolutely had to.'

The so-called Gibson Plan to comprehensively re-construct the city in favour of cars, industry and concrete blocks of flats produced the soulless place we see today. Had the city survived it would have been as popular with tourists as York is today – something Billy himself said on a number of occasions – but when the bombs and, worse, the developers had finished their work, the once beautiful city was left as one of the ugliest urban centres in Europe.

The taste for the past had not yet arrived in England and, like youngsters everywhere, Billy and his friends were not interested in old buildings. They wanted parties and cinemas, bright lights and fun. Coundon could only offer a few old pubs along with acres of dereliction.

But, like all children Billy accepted life as he found it, although at some point in his childhood – and it was unusually early, perhaps around the age of ten – he seems to have become aware that war-damaged Coventry was not for him. He became desperate to get away.

A friend with whom he later fell out, and who did not want to be named, said:

> I knew Billy when he was eleven and all he could talk about was going to London. He hated Coventry because it was so grimy and flat – by flat I mean deadly dull – which it was. There was no romance in the city and life sort of plodded along in a way he hated. We called him

Gentleman Jim because now and then he seemed a bit showy – he had what we called 'airs and graces'. His slightly aloof manner wasn't too obvious and I don't remember him being bullied for it, but he was definitely different. He worried about things such as breaking his nails and was worried about his appearance in a way that other kids definitely were not.

Other friends recalled a boy who developed a closed inner world; a boy who became secretive and a bit of a loner. It would be glib to put this down to his growing realisation of his homosexuality, but that no doubt played a part. Billy's childhood friend Dick Smith lived just a few hundred yards from him in those early years and he stayed in touch after Billy moved to London. He saw him now and then during his first decade at Clarence House. He describes the teenage Billy as having a detached air, always seeming to be on his own, and by the age of fourteen he had certainly lost whatever interest he had once had in the rough and tumble of street games.

I remember the day we all left Barker's Butts School. We were fifteen. At the end of the day we all sat on Billy's wall just chatting about this and that. A few days later and without a word, he'd gone – to London, I mean.

Word quickly spread that Billy had managed to get himself a job in the kitchens at Buckingham Palace. Billy's mother Mabel allegedly dropped it into the conversation whenever she could, but she was vague about what exactly he was doing. Billy's friends thought she was proud of the fact that he'd got himself a job in London but was less pleased that people thought he was working in the kitchens, which she felt was beneath her Billy. And, besides, it was not true.

In the streets of Coundon the words 'Buckingham Palace' had a glamour that made people indifferent to the details.

Dick Smith said, 'We were amazed and, in fact, we didn't believe it at first, but then none of us at that time knew Billy had been writing to the palace for years. That only came out much later when he was well known.'

Chapter Four

Glamorous worlds

BILLY'S LONGING FOR a more glamorous life came to dominate his early teens; but where was this life to be found? Well, surprisingly, Billy found it initially all over the city in the form of newspaper stories and magazine features about the doings of the royal family. Likewise, the radio held a fascination for the young man because it regularly broadcast the voices of the royals, as well as news about their trips around the country and abroad.

The old Bakelite wireless at home where the family would sit and listen to the news became a vital means by which Billy, in his mind at least, could wander far away. And news about the royals was far more uncritical at that time than it later became. Journalists wrote in hugely deferential terms, as if their role were to pay homage to the royals, and that, of course, is in stark contrast to more recent times when journalists began actively to try to uncover damaging stories about them.

But in Billy's early days, radio bulletins would solemnly report the mere fact that the family had travelled from Windsor to Sandringham, or from Buckingham Palace to Balmoral. The tone of reports in those innocent days was one that only hinted at the sort of glamour that so captivated Billy. Here was a world, he thought, that was filled with golden beings far removed from the grime of everyday life in Coventry; beings who travelled the country and the world staying in glamorous places and who were seemingly above criticism, their every move a source of wonder to the British public. Even the coats and dresses worn by the family were described at length in the newspapers and magazines of the time.

So, deeply moved by all that he saw and heard about this glamorous distant world, Billy began, aged about eight, to collect every possible scrap of information he could lay his hands on about the royal family. He filled notebooks with jottings about the family and beautifully kept scrapbooks bulged with cuttings from newspapers and magazines. The old photograph-filled *Picture Post* magazine was a special favourite and where some boys spent their pocket money on sweets and *Hotspur* magazine, Billy tracked down and bought every publication that included photographs of the latest royal visit.

For Billy it didn't matter which royal it was – he collected them all, including pictures and stories about George VI, crowned in 1937, but also Mary of Teck, the late king George V's consort who was to die in 1953. He even collected pictures of Belgian, Spanish and Swedish royalty.

The main focus of Billy's attention was undoubtedly the King and Queen. He knew Elizabeth Bowes-Lyon had married Albert Frederick Arthur George, the future George VI, in 1923, in Westminster Abbey. The wedding was one of the great events of that year with crowds filling Parliament Square, Whitehall and Victoria Street, but, as we have seen, no one at that time had ever imagined that Albert would become king.

Albert was famously shy and retiring; he was a man with an intense dislike of public speaking – he had an appalling stammer – and the various high-profile duties of a monarch filled him with dread. It was the scandal of his brother Edward's relationship with Wallis Simpson and subsequent abdication in 1936 that led to an extraordinary change in the young royal couple's life.

The young Billy was fascinated by this turbulent history, which was still relatively recent news when he was a young man. It was still the greatest scandal of the age.

Meanwhile, as his tiny bedroom walls filled up with grainy black and white photographs and news stories cut from every publication he could lay his hands on, Billy developed what amounted almost to an obsession with the royal family. He would go as far as to fish old magazines out of dustbins to check to see if he had missed a story. In the days when *Picture Post* dominated magazine sales at the newsagents he made sure he secured copies that remained unsold since at that time magazines were ordered on what was called firm sale (rather than sale or return) so Billy knew that if they were not sold by the newsagent they were likely to be thrown away.

By the time he was fifteen Billy had amassed a detailed dossier – almost a miniature library according to one contemporary – of royal lives. The dossier eventually also included stories about distant relatives of the immediate royal family – including stories about the Russian royals – and it covered a period of more than five years.

Billy's interest in the royals was in marked contrast to his interest in school lessons. But then he would have guessed that no amount of study at Barker's Butts would rescue him from his fate. He needed another way out, and so he channelled his considerable intelligence into his royal collection and, by the age of eleven, he knew he wanted to work for the royal family.

WHEN THE COMPTROLLER of the Royal Household at Buckingham Palace received a carefully written, if slightly clumsily composed letter postmarked Coventry and addressed directly to George VI, he must have been tempted to throw it into the waste paper basket.

The letter would have arrived in 1947 or early 1948. It explained that the writer was a huge fan of the royal family, was intelligent and hardworking, loyal, conscientious and honest. The writer explained all his good qualities and then asked if he could have a job – any job – at the palace.

Having sent that letter the young Billy Tallon waited, desperately hoping for a positive reply. The King's office almost certainly did reply, but it was inevitably a gentle brush off, as Billy was too young to leave school. Undaunted, Billy wrote every six months or so from then on, always politely suggesting that as soon as he was able to leave school he would like to work in the royal household.

At school, as the time for leaving aged fifteen approached, the other boys played football and made paper aeroplanes in lessons while Billy dreamed of a new life far away. He later told a friend that, much as he loved his family, especially his mother Mabel, he felt he did not have any really close friends as a child. Towards the end of his life, Billy said:

> I was different, definitely. All the boys at my school loved football
> and Airfix models, or they played in the street as most kids did at that
> time. I used to play occasionally but my heart wasn't in it. I suppose it
> was rather odd that my only interest pretty much was the royal family,
> but you have to remember that for me they represented a wonderful,
> exotic world that I wanted to be part of. There wasn't much that was
> glamorous about Coventry then. Nobody ever seemed to do anything

interesting. Frankly, I couldn't wait to get away. But how was it to be done? That's what troubled me.

Barker's Butts did put many children in for what used to be called CSE exams. CSE stood for Certificate of Secondary Education, a well-intentioned attempt to find some way to recognise the achievements of children who were deemed non-academic. CSE passes were really worth little more than the paper they were written on. Employers knew straight away that an applicant for a job with CSEs rather than O-levels was a child who had failed so far as education was concerned. Billy knew they were worthless and never sat for them.

Though not academic in the conventional sense, Billy was intelligent enough to know that the school could not give him the start in life he wanted, so the letter writing to Buckingham Palace – he always addressed his letters to the palace – continued as he moved toward his fifteenth year when he could leave school.

As luck would have it, around this time one of his letters struck a chord with someone in the royal household. Instead of the usual reply, something new and exciting arrived in the post. Billy himself said on several occasions in later life that he had written to the royals so often partly because he really did hope to get a job but also because he loved the thick embossed envelopes that came back carrying each reply.

The early letters had all thanked him for his interest but regretfully informed him that there were no vacancies. These replies and their envelopes were carefully added to his collection of royal memorabilia. Billy never regarded them as depressing rejections; they were simply part of a delightful link to a world he longed to be part of.

But then that very different letter arrived.

It asked Billy to present himself to the Comptroller of the Royal Household as soon as he could. Clearly the endless series of letters had paid off because the interview, as Billy later recalled, turned out to be a mere formality.

He had been terrified he would get lost so he deliberately caught a very early train and then wandered about for more than two hours in Green Park, with Buckingham Palace always in view, until it was time to approach a policeman, show his letter and be taken to the side of the palace and in through the servants' door.

Having had his duties explained to him – opening doors, general fetching and carrying and being obedient to the senior footmen – Billy was sent on his way.

Billy's mother was delighted when his return to Coventry was quickly followed by a letter confirming that they really had decided to give her son a job. She too saw royal service as a cut above the rest. She was part of a generation that almost venerated the royals and from having been doubtful that Billy would ever be taken on, she was as astonished as Billy himself when the invitation to the interview and then the acceptance letter landed on the doorstep. She was a proud woman and quickly let it be known among the neighbours that Billy was off to London to the royal household. Her son would not be working in the local factories after all.

Mabel coughed up the cost of the train fare and a short while after the letter had arrived Billy packed his little bag – he had one set of spare clothes, some stamps and pen and paper with which to write home – and caught the train back to London to start his new life.

I had been so enthusiastic about joining the staff that I think it was probably a foregone conclusion that I would get the job. I mean, I wasn't exactly bad looking and I think they had a sixth sense about when a person would fit in well. At the time, I thought I was in heaven and was terrified they might still turn me down. Looking back of course I realised I had got it all out of proportion. I mean, I was only hoping to get the most menial job – I'd have taken anything they'd offered and for those lowly jobs of course the household itself couldn't afford to be too choosy.

Always devoted to his mother, he promised to write and return home when he got the chance, but typically he didn't say goodbye to any of the boys he had known either at school or in the neighbouring houses. Billy's focus had always been elsewhere and the truth is that he had no particularly close friends among the other Coundon boys. His growing awareness of his homosexuality – still then illegal – no doubt intensified his natural instinct to reticence and secrecy, an instinct that years of royal service would only intensify.

Billy wrote home soon after arriving at the palace to say that he had his own little room and had just had tea which consisted of 'eggs and chips followed by jelly'. He loved his family but there was no note of missing them at all in this or in subsequent letters. So far as Billy was concerned, he had finally arrived where he was always destined to be.

Chapter Five

Below stairs

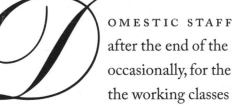OMESTIC STAFF WERE difficult to find after the end of the Second World War, even, occasionally, for the royals. The war had given the working classes broader horizons and the 'shame and tyranny of the maid's cap', as it was known, made many girls and boys seek better-paid and less humiliating factory work. But, despite this, the number of domestic staff employed by the royals in the late 1940s was far higher than in more recent times,

when public scrutiny and questions about taxpayer value made one or two members of the royal family wary of seeming to enjoy the attentions of an almost medieval retinue of staff. As we have seen, there were exceptions to this; most notably the Queen Mother.

Like the upper and middle classes, the royals tried in principle to make do with fewer servants as the 1940s and 1950s wore on. People who had grown up without the faintest notion of how to make a cup of tea or boil an egg, who had had everything done for them, found they could no longer afford the teams of servants they had once taken for granted unless they were prepared to pay the sort of wages offered elsewhere. Those they had relied upon for so long were gradually drifting away and those who remained in service had to be treated with far more respect than had previously been the case.

It was almost as if there had been a subtle power shift. Elderly aristocratic women were terrified the cook would leave because they knew it would be difficult if not impossible to find a replacement. In the past, the cook would not have been able to leave for alternative employment because there was none. But times had changed and well-paid factory and office jobs were always beckoning. The days when servants had no alternative were over.

But if servants' conditions generally were improving around the time Billy started work, there was still a sense in which changes in royal service always came later than elsewhere.

For junior members of staff – hall boys, junior footmen and kitchen maids – royal palaces were divided strictly. Generally speaking, they were told never to leave their immediate areas of work. It was forbidden for any servant to use the main staircase in the house unless they were given special permission and, above all, no servant was permitted to speak to a member of the family in the unlikely event of meeting one of them.

Junior servants were also told that under no circumstances should they address remarks or queries to the senior servants. The maids always reported to the housekeeper – and addressed any queries to her – while the junior staff, including the hall boys, reported to those immediately above them in the hierarchy, never to the butler. As a contemporary of Billy's at Clarence House recalled:

> You have to remember that big houses were designed to ensure as little contact as possible between servants and their employers. It was a very strict rule, but strict rules existed at every level – that's why I couldn't speak to the butler or the cook. I was too lowly and even the servants wanted their status.

Of course, the top of the servant tree was always working for the royal household. For the career minded, work in a royal palace was just a stepping stone to highly paid work overseas – for rich Americans or other wealthy foreigners who were always dazzled if a servant they hoped to employ had previously worked for the British royal family.

But, however impressed outsiders might have been, the truth remained that, in the palace, servant work was pretty much the same as it was in any other large house: it was a daily grind of cleaning, tidying up, preparing meals, laying tables and standing around waiting for orders.

⁓ ✺ ⁓

*B*ILLY HAD BEEN offered a job as a junior steward or footman at £2 a week. The key elements of the junior steward's job included opening and closing doors, cleaning shoes, running errands and, above all, remaining invisible.

The pay may have seemed meagre but the job included accommodation, food and a new suit of clothes each year. Billy would have known that if he worked hard and blended into the background he might be promoted. Best of all, of course, he had arrived where he had always wanted to be, and it was not a disappointment.

> I was very nervous it is true, so nervous that my first few days are now a blur, but I worked on the simple principle that I would do whatever I was told to do promptly and without arguing. And I made sure I was absolutely immaculately dressed from the very first day. I realised that smartness was very important to the royal family so I spent a long time each morning in front of the mirror!

A servant who started work in the early 1930s in a large house just a few hundred yards from Buckingham Palace recalled the atmosphere of those times:

> On my first day at Spencer House I was told that on my afternoon off each Tuesday I was to go home to my family and not to talk to any other servant who was having a half day on the same day, neither a

servant from Spencer House nor from any other house round about. I was also told that meeting friends on my day off was not allowed. I didn't quite understand, but since I had no friends outside a tiny area of Paddington I thought I could probably ignore this advice!

The ban on talking to servants from other houses was strictly enforced so far as possible because families employing many servants – and especially the royal family – hated the idea that their secrets should be spread abroad, and there was a class-based idea that the lower orders were addicted to gossip.

Of course, the risk of family secrets becoming the talk of the town was greatly exaggerated. It is difficult to imagine that a kitchen maid would discover anything of any real interest – except perhaps to other servants. It was felt that servants were a necessity but a problematic one. They had to be allowed lives of their own, but had to be kept under control; at the same time they mustn't be treated so harshly that they would leave. This created an atmosphere of discipline and rigid hierarchy that many found stifling. Billy, on the other hand, loved order and discipline.

In these very early days Billy would have been aware of legendary figures such as Walter Taylor, who was then Groom of the Backstairs, a highly regarded post to which Billy would eventually be appointed when Walter died in 1978. Almost nothing is known of Taylor beyond the fact that he was discretion personified and hugely popular with everyone in the royal household.

'He was a remarkable man: solid and dependable; friendly but not given to gossip. He knew the job inside out and had a knack of always being in the right place at the right time in terms of making sure the royals got what they wanted. There was something almost uncanny about him!' remembered a contemporary. Taylor seems to have been the model on which, at least from a professional point of view, Billy based his own career.

In the heady below-stairs atmosphere at Buckingham Palace Billy quickly learned who was important and who was not. He was ambitious from the start, which surprised many of his colleagues. One said:

> Well, Billy's family had run a shop but the shop had failed and he grew up in an environment of loss and failure; an environment where people had fairly low expectations. But Billy was different. From his first day at the palace his sights were high, perhaps because he did not want to repeat his own family's financial failure. He was determined not to fail. He wanted to live up to his mother's expectations and not fall through the cracks as Mabel, Billy's mother, seems to have felt her husband, William, had done.

Billy had been very much the odd man out at home in Coundon and at Buckingham Palace something of this feeling remained. He felt he was somehow different from the other servants. Certainly he was part of the below-stairs team, yet he was a cut above the kitchen and domestic staff. He always felt destined for higher things. He had enormous amounts of what we would now call self-belief. It was something all his colleagues and friends noticed.

Those in lower jobs and who perhaps saw no way of rising disliked their jobs in a way that would have surprised Billy. Peter Livesey, who worked in the kitchens at the palace, is probably typical.

> In the kitchens at Buckingham Palace we hated it because our chances of promotion were precisely zero; we were menials, far lower in a way than the junior footmen. We washed up and stacked dishes and kept the place clean – that was it.
>
> People higher up had to die before you could take their place, so to make up for the low wages some people would even steal the spoons and anything else they could get their hands on!

Peter also recalled some of the lighter moments in the royal kitchens, where, as in many grand houses, different kitchens were used to produce different parts of a meal. At breakfast, for example, the toast was made in the coffee room while the eggs were made one hundred yards away in another kitchen. In the mornings as a result footmen were regularly seen racing along the corridors holding aloft plates of toast (or going in the opposite direction with eggs) desperately hoping everything would stay warm until it reached the breakfast table. Occasionally two footmen would collide and eggs and toast would hurtle in various directions.

But with low wages and better-paid employment elsewhere, the palace was forced to employ pretty much anyone in some of the most menial jobs in the late 1950s and 1960s. Servants had become so hard to find that desperation sometimes led to wildly inappropriate appointments, as Peter Livesey recalled: 'You'd often find yourself working next to someone who had been in prison, and someone like that would spend the whole time looking for stuff to nick and then one day they wouldn't turn up for work and you'd find loads of silver missing.'

It was too time consuming and expensive to check up on everyone and employment agencies were under similar pressure: to stay in business they had to place people and it was in their interest not to ask too many questions. It was a huge security risk but there seemed little alternative at the time.

For the royal household this presented a number of difficulties, chief of which was the need for discretion. When there were problems in the kitchen they kept quiet about thefts of spoons and tongs and odd bits of silver, even though they were valuable, simply because they didn't want the publicity.

As Peter Livesey puts it:

> They didn't want people to know they'd employed some really dodgy characters! They were caught in a double bind: if they went for decent people it would cost more, and they might not be able to find anyone at all because the turnover of staff was so high, but if they publicised thefts by bringing a prosecution now and then, it might encourage others to try to get work in the kitchens solely to try to steal things.

It was widely known in those pre-vetting days that ex-offenders often found their way into jobs in the royal kitchens. Livesey remembers 'at least one murderer who had been released after a decade in the nick'.

The fact is that, with a few exceptions, royal service was a dead end, and a low-paid dead end at that. In some staff this created a lingering sense of anger and Livesey recalls one ex-offender spitting in a dish that was being prepared for a group of distinguished visitors. Kitchen work was also seen as women's work and there was no tradition of rising from the kitchen as there was if you were a footman like Billy. Even junior footmen could expect to appear before members of the family occasionally and if the family liked them they were promoted. It was as simple as that. Meanwhile although it is true that Cook might get some recognition if the food was really good – and Cook was the best-paid member of the kitchen team – there was nonetheless a tradition that kept the kitchen staff entirely separate from those for whom they worked.

Livesey explains:

> I think they never gave a thought to the people in the kitchen. All their lives, servants had provided for them so they took it for granted. They thought it was like magic. Poof – every day three meals appeared before their very eyes! Poof – their beds were made! Poof – their socks were washed.

But Peter also recalled that the kitchen could be fun. There was a sense of camaraderie and there were rules that were so absurd that they lightened even the dullest days.

For example, whenever there was a banquet at Buckingham Palace, all the potatoes and sprouts, carrots and other vegetables had to be measured before being served to make sure they were of similar dimensions and would not spoil the appearance of the dinner table.

'I used to wonder what on earth taxpayers would think,' remembers Livesey.

And, by any standards the rewards of domestic service were dire, as the wage and salary list for 2006 reveals: footmen and housemaids started on a salary of around £13,500 a year. On promotion to senior footman, that might rise to around £15,500. Things were slightly better for a butler who would start on around £15,000, plus accommodation, but it is easy to imagine how difficult it would be to live in London on these shockingly small sums.

In addition to poor wages, servants had to put up with some appallingly menial work. A former palace servant who did not want to be named, but who worked as a hall boy for several years, recalled cleaning not only the royal household's shoes but those of the upper servants, a perk Billy Tallon was later to enjoy:

> My job meant endless boot and shoe cleaning, and I can tell you that footwear had to be absolutely gleaming or boots and shoes would come flying back – quite literally hurled at my head by a senior footman.
>
> I sometimes did Prince Philip's shoes but mostly I was cleaning the upper servants' shoes and boots. I did the butlers' and the footmen's, but not the junior footmen's – they had to do their own! Together with the scullery maid I also had to empty the chamber pots every morning – you'd hardly believe it but some of the royals didn't like traipsing along the corridors to the loos at night, so they used chamber pots well into the 1960s.

⚬ ⚬ ⚬

*B*ILLY HAD SEVERAL great advantages over the other servants in his early days at Buckingham Palace. Chief among these were his good looks and his explicitly stated determination to stay for life. He already knew a great deal about the royal family and was so eager to learn how to be a good servant that he was quickly marked down as the sort of person who should be kept on if at all possible. The equerries and other senior advisers knew by this time that it was very difficult to get footmen and butlers who were discreet and well mannered and who could be convinced to stay in the job for life – not to mention work up to seventy hours a week.

Employment agencies such as Greycoats were always trying to poach staff for other wealthy clients – who would invariably pay more than the notoriously stingy royals – and it became at times a struggle to get good people and to get them to stay. In later life Billy was regularly approached with immensely lucrative offers of work in America. He always refused even to discuss the possibility.

But the problem for the palace in those early days when Billy first came to London was that, apart from low wages, work in the royal household was based on a regime that regularly asked its employees to work twelve-hour days, six or even seven days a week. Billy made his mark early because he didn't mind this at all. His other great advantages were that he was tall, handsome and extremely attentive.

53

A friend who knew him in his junior footman days recalled another of his remarkable qualities:

> He was always there but in the background whenever Queen Elizabeth, later the Queen Mother, was having lunch or dinner or needed anything. It was an uncanny ability to be right where they needed him, when they needed him. I know how he learned to do this – he watched Walter Taylor, who was then still Groom of the Backstairs, as if his life depended on it. You could see where Billy had almost absorbed the mannerisms, the style and even the way Walter walked.
>
> Billy worked for various members of the family in those early days in Buckingham Palace. He just had a gift for the work. They all wanted him. He was ornamental – I mean classically tall, dark and handsome – and the royal household knew even as early as 1950 that he was probably going to be happy to spend almost all his time at the palace and at work. He was always available and rarely asked for time off.

Billy himself acknowledged his debt to Walter Taylor:

> He was a great model for any young servant. He had a presence and a kind of dignified bearing that was as impressive in its way as anything demonstrated by the royals themselves.
>
> But I'm not sure anyone would say that they liked Walter – in the sense of feeling close to him – because he was aloof. He never let his guard down, but he was immensely impressive. He had an air of greatness – I don't think it would be too much to say that.

But, whatever the influence of below-stairs events, it was changes in the wider world that transformed Billy's life. The death of Queen Elizabeth's husband King George VI in 1952 was the catalyst that began the young footman's meteoric rise to the top – the first major consequence being the widowed Queen's removal from Buckingham Palace to Clarence House in 1953. This left Buckingham Palace free for the newly crowned Queen Elizabeth, her husband Prince Philip, her young family and, of course, her servants.

Chapter Six

The shy King

THE SECOND SON of George V, Albert Frederick Arthur George Saxe-Coburg-Gotha – known to the family as Bertie – was not, as we have seen, expected to become king. It was the abdication of his brother Edward VIII in 1936 that changed everything, and the details of Edward's love affair with twice-married Wallis Simpson are so well known as not to need repeating.

The fact was, however, that the abdication pushed what was

essentially a very shy man into one of the most high-profile roles in the world, and this inevitably had a profound effect on the woman he had married in 1923. It has been said on good authority that Elizabeth, later the Queen Mother, never forgave Edward or his wife Mrs Simpson for putting personal relationships before duty. In 1939, she wrote to Prince Paul of Yugoslavia, 'The mass of people do not forgive quickly the sort of thing that he [the Duke of Windsor] did to this country. And they hate her.'

Elizabeth believed, rightly or wrongly, that being thrust into the limelight hastened her husband's death. The fact that he was a heavy, lifelong smoker who had had a lung removed some time prior to his death was of course the more immediate cause of his demise, but, whatever the case, it seems undeniable that Elizabeth was deeply in love with Bertie as well as being highly protective of him. He had put duty before his own health, as she saw it, where Edward and Mrs Simpson had put their happiness before duty.

WHEN ALBERT WAS crowned in Westminster Abbey in May 1937 he took the regnal name George VI. From then on he was under enormous pressure to stamp his authority on the role. He knew he would inevitably be compared to his hugely popular brother who, as Prince of Wales, was cheered wildly by crowds wherever his tours took him. But the new king simply did not have Edward's charisma, although he tried hard to make the best of the situation.

Elizabeth's attitude to Bertie throughout these early years of his reign tells us a great deal about her relationships with men in general and, later on, with Billy. She was intensely loyal and supportive, but only perhaps because Bertie relied on her totally. Had he been more aloof and independent – less reliant on her advice and support – she would have responded in kind. William Tallon was always aware of this: where she found loyalty, she reflected it back. Where she found indifference, she reflected indifference.

Bertie was a quiet, diffident man who, like so many royal males, knew that he really didn't have to try hard in life. The triumph and the tragedy of his life was that, prior to his brother's abdication, he was destined for a life of luxury and idleness with the additional benefit that he could live this life well out of the public gaze. He had been trained, as it were, to expect this; it was implicit in his upbringing. Then, against all the odds, to find himself doing something for which he was singularly unsuited – and untrained – almost certainly outweighed all the advantages of royal birth.

He was neither ambitious nor particularly driven to succeed in any area of life. He had been allowed to enter the Naval College at Osborne on the Isle of Wight in 1911 despite not being 'officer material', either by personality or by inclination. He entered as a naval cadet but fared so badly that he came bottom of his class in the final examinations. The trouble may have had more to do with lack of ambition than lack of intelligence, or it may have been simply that Bertie knew that his life would remain the same whether he tried hard or not. This is something that invariably affects members of the royal family, but in different ways. It perhaps reached its nadir when in more recent times Prince Charles was offered a place at Cambridge University despite A-level grades that would have led to rejection for any other candidate.

During his Isle of Wight days, Bertie was known by fellow crew members as 'Mr Johnson'. He served aboard HMS *Collingwood* during the First World War and was mentioned in despatches during the Battle of Jutland (May 1916–June 1916). He spent the rest of the war recovering from an ulcer operation and then entered Trinity College, Cambridge for a year. He seems to have gone to Cambridge much as he went to the naval college: he was sent there with few academic qualifications simply because he had nothing better to do.

After his early years spent somehow drifting through life, Bertie's marriage to Elizabeth Bowes-Lyon came as a surprise. It showed that he was prepared occasionally to kick over the traces and make a decision that seemed out of character – and, strictly speaking, outside the rules.

❧

*I*T WAS CLEARLY a love match. Although an aristocrat, Elizabeth Bowes-Lyon was not royalty and indeed she was apparently so appalled at the prospect of marrying Bertie and becoming a member of a family so much under the spotlight that when he first proposed in 1921 she turned him down. She hated the idea that she would no longer be able to think and speak for herself – an astute comment on the nature of life in Britain's most famous family.

But Bertie was so besotted that he told everyone, including his mother Queen Mary, that if he could not marry Elizabeth he would not marry at all. The story goes that Queen Mary was so concerned that she visited Glamis Castle in Scotland to meet Elizabeth and speak to her privately. Mary was apparently so impressed that she immediately gave her permission for the match – if Bertie could prevail. There was clearly some indefinable strength combined with gentleness in Elizabeth that appealed to the vulnerable Bertie. And there is no doubt that Elizabeth had had other offers. For several years after the war she had been pursued by equerry James Stuart and had he not gone to America to earn his fortune, Elizabeth might well have married him rather than Bertie.

There are clear parallels between Elizabeth's almost maternal affection for her shy, stuttering, unambitious husband and Queen Victoria's affection for Prince Albert. Victoria's love for Albert was reflected in forty years of mourning – Victoria wore black for the rest of her life after Albert's premature death in 1861 and the country, monarchist to a degree impossible to imagine today, followed suit. Black clocks, black suits, dark furniture and dark interiors became the norm due to the all-pervasive influence of the Queen. Indeed, the dark clouds didn't lift until 1901, when Victoria died.

But behind the public mourning and elevation of Albert to a status of quasi sainthood, Victoria, as we have seen, appears to have fallen in love with someone else after her husband's death: her servant John Brown. Victoria could never re-marry (at least not if it became public knowledge) but needed a close relationship with a man – likewise Elizabeth Bowes-Lyon. When Albert – George VI – died in 1952, aged just fifty-six, there is no doubting Elizabeth's genuine distress. She didn't quite go into a lifetime of mourning as Victoria had done, but she similarly needed male company – without any risk that she might compromise her status as national treasure by provoking rumours that she might re-marry.

It is easy to forget the peculiar difficulties under which many members of the royal family labour. The revolution of the past few decades that has seen three out of four of the Queen's children divorce would have been unthinkable back in the 1940s and 1950s, which is why the King's abdication in 1936 was such a shock. It was the idea of the King trying to marry someone who would have been perfectly acceptable to the establishment if she had remained his mistress that was unacceptable.

So, when George VI died in 1952 Elizabeth knew she would have to reconcile herself to a life without a partner. It was a question of being seen to remain loyal to the dead king, just as Victoria had remained loyal, at least publicly, to Albert. A new relationship for the monarch's mother would have been viewed as unseemly, so Elizabeth had to reconcile herself to a life of loneliness, a life without intimacy.

Of course, to some extent her whole upbringing was about learning to live without intimacy; instead it was about learning to live surrounded by servants and advisers with barely a moment of solitude from morning till night.

But Elizabeth had enjoyed her relationship with Bertie and hated the fact that she could never again enjoy a similar relationship of real closeness. This is why she threw herself into a lifetime of dinner parties and lunch parties; why she travelled from one royal residence to another; and most especially why she relished the company of Billy Tallon.

There is no record of Elizabeth having a long close relationship with any female servant nor with a man who was not an adviser or servant; in other words with someone who was not 'safe' because he was effectively employed by her. Billy was to Elizabeth what John Brown was to Victoria.

Despite the difficulties of her position and her public persona, Elizabeth was determined to have fun. Very determined. Her resourcefulness and force of character is nowhere better illustrated than in her reaction to the death of her husband. Within weeks of her daughter Elizabeth becoming queen, the widowed Elizabeth decamped to Clarence House a few hundred yards along the Mall and here she was to remain for the rest of her life. She took the title Queen Mother, a title entirely of her own invention and without historic precedent, and she managed to create a court to rival that of her daughter. It was a remarkable achievement but it depended very largely on the public perception that she had sacrificed her own pleasure and her own personal life for the country. Privately, of course, she had a whale of a time.

Where Elizabeth II seemed to be everything a queen should be – regal, aloof, dignified and impeccably well behaved – her mother created a role for herself as a sort of royal grande dame. She always seemed slightly softer and less detached than her daughter, more willing to engage with the emotions of the crowd rather than simply

acknowledging their adoration. And of course everyone remembered that she had insisted on remaining in London during the
worst of the Blitz. It was all part of an image that was brilliantly
created and maintained, and Billy was a central part of that image.

*B*ILLY HAD BEEN working at Buckingham Palace for
just over a year when Elizabeth found herself a widow.
He was still a junior footman, whose duties were as mundane as
they had been when he started work, but as a contemporary and
fellow royal servant recalled, he had already distinguished himself.

I remember Billy coming along a corridor and thinking 'that bloke
will go far' – he had a mimic's genius for taking on the airs of his betters. I don't mean that he was affected, it was never as crude as that,
but he absorbed their manners and mannerisms in a very subtle way
– the way a child in the playground would absorb a new language. It
all became second nature to him. At first I thought it might lead to
trouble – I mean 'aping your betters' as they used to say, but I realised
that Billy absorbed only enough of upper-class ways to avoid saying
things that might irritate them.

He never said 'phone' or 'toilet', which someone from his background
might have said. He always said 'napkin', not 'serviette'; 'writing paper',
not 'note paper'; 'looking glass', not 'mirror'. Most of the royals', and
especially the equerries', ears were primed for this sort of thing – if
you used the wrong word they could place you, as it were ('dreadfully

common') – but Billy was so quick to lose his northern accent and instinctively to know which word to use that within a few years he was a figure even the grandest equerries could not quite place.

Of course, everyone knew all about Billy's origins and the fact that he was a footman and later groom meant they also knew he was not, as it were, out of the top drawer as they themselves inevitably were, but his ambiguous nature often made them slightly uneasy. Even when Billy made a mistake it was often a mistake that did his career no harm at all. In his first year, for example, he gave the Queen Mother a postal order for seven shillings and sixpence on her birthday. He was given a good telling off and the money was returned, but it is hard to imagine that the Queen Mother was not touched by the gesture. She must have noticed this oddly deferential boy who was so eager to please yet so dignified at the same time. It was around this time too that Billy first came to the attention of the equerries when the Queen Mother asked about her 'rather dashing young footman'.

Billy was always rather vague about this early period, but it seems as if he really was noticed at first because he looked the part, rather than because he was especially efficient at his daily duties. 'Looking the part' may not sound a particularly important part of a footman's duties, but fifty or sixty years earlier it had been standard procedure in many grand houses to measure the calves of applicants for footmen's jobs. A good calf was seen as absolutely essential as recently as the 1880s because footmen were not just employed to work; they were also status symbols and ornaments.

James Lees, who worked as a footman in a number of grand houses, recalled the importance of appearance:

> My first boss, who had started work as a junior footman in one of the London palaces at the end of the nineteenth century, was a fascinating character who loved telling me about how things were done when he first began in service. After working for a number of years in a very lowly position, he had applied for a job elsewhere as a footman proper. Satisfactory references were forthcoming and as there was no stigma attached to the desire to change jobs he was full of confidence when he presented himself for interview. But the interview was a very odd experience. It began with the senior butler staring at him for ten minutes without saying a word and then asking the young man to walk about the room while he continued to stare. He then asked a series of very general questions about former duties before suddenly standing up and leaving the room without a word of explanation. Five more minutes elapsed before he returned with an extremely elderly and rather unsteady man in tow. This second man appeared to be dressed in the fashion of the late Georgian period! Having done *his* share of staring, the doddery old chap pulled a strange looking pair of callipers out of his pocket and then knelt at the young applicant's feet. He applied the callipers to the boy's calves, staggered back up, said, 'He'll do!' and promptly left the room.

Echoes of these ancient practices would have survived into Billy's time in the junior footman's room. In addition, the sheer numbers of servants employed across the country is now hard to comprehend.

In fact, Billy's first year in royal service was characterised by a regime that is today all but unrecognisable. Even relatively modest semi-detached houses in London's suburbs might still have a live-in maid at the time and the dowagers of Mayfair would have teams of servants in houses that are now almost all offices.

For servants there were very strict rules, as Stephen Rhodes, a butler for more than forty years in a number of London houses, recalled:

> As hall boy, garden boy, footman, valet and butler, I had to put up with all sorts of nonsense from the people I worked for – childish behaviour, tantrums and ridiculous demands at all hours of the day and night, and often for things you wouldn't like to tell your mother about! There was also a lot of sexual abuse of the female servants – and God help any particularly pretty maid!

The difficulty with the servant–master relationship was traditionally that all the power was on one side. Aristocratic young men using their power to press for sexual favours from a pretty maid is a literary commonplace. In the upstairs–downstairs relationship, maids and footmen, even butlers and more senior staff, could traditionally be dismissed at a moment's notice. Of course, there were always many exceptions to the rule that servants were generally not treated well – Queen Victoria, for example, famously sacked her favourite chef, Charles Elmé Francatelli, after hearing that he had hit one of her maids. But in the grand scheme of things, servants simply had to do what they were told, even if the demands were unreasonable. This is the background against which we have to see Billy's long years of royal service.

The other side of the equation was that servants often grew to be very close to the men and women by whom they were employed. This is especially true of the period in which Billy worked; one in which the power relationship was gradually changing. Stephen Rhodes's memories confirm this: 'Later in my career the barriers seemed to come down completely and employers began to treat me as if I was a friend. They'd sometimes be terrified if you told them you were leaving and would do almost anything to keep you.'

Being dependent on servants for everything – once a sign of prestige – had become a sign of vulnerability because those servants could simply leave and get work in the burgeoning world of manufacturing and commerce. Servants who stayed often did so because a curious kind of mutual dependence had grown up between them and those for whom they worked. The financial rewards never amounted to much but there were compensations for those who worked their way up the promotion ladder. For Billy, as for so many male servants, the initial aim was to become a butler – the aristocrats of the servant world. Stephen Rhodes recalled 'a good butler was supposed to be deaf and blind'.

> For example, I had to pretend not to know anything about it when my boss slipped along the corridor and went into another man's wife's bedroom, but since they were all at it I suppose it didn't much signify.

But it was worth being discreet as the butler was the best-paid servant in the house and the less you saw and heard the bigger the tips!

Butlers also lived in the best of the servants' rooms or they might be
offered a cottage or a flat if an employer was particularly well off. In
royal service a butler or any other senior servant would be treated
with great respect by the lower servants, by tradesmen and by visitors.

In his first job as a junior footman, however, Billy could only
dream of future possibilities. He was the lowest of the upper servants, above only the kitchen and garden staff in terms of status.

Early on Billy adopted the royal policy of 'never complain, never
explain', but despite this stoicism, deep down he never forgave
one or two of the equerries and advisers for treating him, as he
saw it, like dirt. His dislike of Sir Alastair Aird, one of the senior
equerries, stems from the 1960s. Aird was a grandee – educated at
Eton and Sandhurst – who loathed what he saw as Billy's inappropriate and growing intimacy with the Queen Mother. But
whatever harsh remarks he had to put up with in his early days,
Billy bided his time. He kept his head down and got on with the
job, despite knowing that further up the hierarchy he was already
marked down as 'a little too full of himself'.

His duties at this time would have been identical to those of
a junior assistant in the steward's room a generation earlier. One
former junior assistant recalled life there in the 1930s:

My day as junior assistant started at five o'clock. We never had an
alarm clock but when you have to get up in the morning it is surprising

how quick you learn to do it automatically. I'd hop out of my bed, get a piece of bread and butter if there was any from the kitchen and eat it as quickly as I could because staff breakfast was later.

As I went along the staff corridors I noticed the walls were dotted here and there with old oil paintings – presumably these were pictures that the family had gone off or they'd been told they were valueless. One showed cattle coming down to a lake in the mountains to drink. It was beautifully done but perhaps a little unfashionable, which is why it had ended up here among the servants. The royals never threw anything away but pictures often went from the drawing room to an old passage and then to the servants' corridors!

The various maids were always already at work when I arrived and made my way to the servants' hall, which was just a big room where the servants ate round a giant table. There was a laundry room, butler's pantry and endless other rooms including, of course, the wine cellar and spirit room – the servants' part of Buckingham Palace takes up a lot of the basement. I was never allowed in the butler's pantry at first because this is where all the solid silver the royals ate off was kept.

In my day as junior assistant I also had to serve breakfast, lunch and dinner to the upper servants.

The day-to-day practical duties of the below-stairs world at Buckingham Palace were enlivened by gossip and there were always rumours about the royals, especially the minor members of the family, and the royal hangers-on. Billy later recalled 'one old lunatic' who was always at Buckingham Palace but no one – certainly not the servants – had a clue who he was or why he was there.

Rumour had it that he was a retired butler, now in his eighties, but no one seemed able to remember. The royals let it be known that the old man was not to be questioned or hindered in any way, as a fellow servant recalled:

> Every January he was reputed to give up smoking and drinking and to walk around with half a raw cabbage in his pocket. Whenever he was hungry he would whip out the cabbage and take a bite. He was very eccentric, but was more or less part of the furniture!

Such figures were not uncommon. They seemed to have lived forever in odd parts of the palace – in 'forgotten corridors and abandoned landings' – and there was a general awareness that they were a permanent fixture. They were almost certainly elderly servants such as the eccentric described above, who had retired but been allowed, unofficially, to stay on.

If Billy and the other key servants did not always go to Royal Lodge, they were obliged to go often to Balmoral where the Queen and Queen Mother might stay for weeks at a time in the summer. Though there was always a permanent team of servants at Balmoral it was not a big enough team to ensure the Queen Mother was properly looked after. As a result, that relatively small team was sometimes supplemented by Billy, the Queen Mother's personal maid and a number of other staff.

But both at Balmoral and elsewhere there were odd groups of servants who seemed to occupy a place somewhere vaguely between the upper servants – aristocrats like Alastair Aird who hated to think of themselves as servants – and the lowly foot-men and maids.

Peter Baker, who worked for a short while at Balmoral, recalled this strange army of misfits.

> They were well-spoken elderly men and women who seemed to occupy rooms that had once been servants' rooms, but they never did any work. In fact they never did anything. They were waited on by the other serv-ants and everyone assumed they were either retired ladies in waiting or distant relatives of the royal family who no one knew what to do with. We used to joke that we were paying for them through our taxes.
>
> We didn't mind the royals themselves but why these others? I think myself they were probably cousins or second cousins of some jun-ior branch of the family and they were so eccentric that the only way to prevent them embarrassing the family was to keep them well fed, well housed and well out of the way. I think the family was worried that there would be another huge scandal of the kind that erupted in the 1970s when it was discovered that one or two of the Queen Mother's close female relatives had spent their whole lives in psychi-atric hospitals.

Other servants remembered similar eccentrics at Windsor. Here three very well-spoken but decidedly odd sisters who appeared to have worked their whole lives at Royal Lodge had been kept on years after anyone could even remember what they had once done. At least one was virtually bed-ridden and could only get about slowly using a frame. No one had a clue what they did or what they had ever done but no one dared to suggest to the Queen Mother that their position should at least be looked at.

And there were oddities too at Clarence House. Here many of the older servants remembered that in the 1950s a junior footman who might or might not have once actually worked in the house appeared still to live there (in the basement) despite not having been officially on the books for several years. The Queen Mother would not hear of his being removed.

The tradition of looking after servants could extend even further – at Windsor, for example, in the 1980s, the royal household built a small bungalow for a retired gamekeeper.

But the situation became untenable when in the mid-1980s the newspapers expressed outrage when it was discovered that many distant relatives of the royal family and former ladies in waiting were living entirely free of charge in grace-and-favour apartments funded by the taxpayer. Many of these were at Hampton Court. The uproar led to changes in the way the apartments were allocated.

But the three sisters at Windsor were long dead by the time the grace-and-favour apartments story hit the headlines. They belonged to an earlier era when loyal servants could expect to be looked after for life. It was all a far cry from the treatment later meted out to Backstairs Billy, who, when describing his experiences of Queen Elizabeth's elderly maids, explained:

> I can remember meeting several old ladies with walking sticks who claimed they were still maids but it was clear that they were far too frail to do any work at all. It was part of Elizabeth's kindness that she

couldn't bear to treat her former servants harshly, especially if they had nowhere else to go.

In view of Billy's bitterness at how he felt he was treated by the royal household at the end of his own career, his words were deeply ironic. But for now the junior footmen had shoes to polish and fires to light, as a contemporary of Billy's recalled:

My first job when I got into the hall at about ten past five was to go to the boot room and start cleaning. A maid would leave the shoes there. We used a special beeswax cream that came in big tins but mostly it was spit and polish and elbow grease – you got a good shine by really going over the leather well with brushes and then cloths. If they weren't absolutely perfect there was hell to pay. But the boots were only the beginning – in fact it was the easy bit because at least I could sit on a stool to do it. Once the boots were cleaned the fun really started!

It used to make me laugh that members of the royal family wouldn't even give the fire a poke to liven it up. They would always ring for the footman to do it and of course to put more logs on the fire. Sometimes a footman would spend the whole evening standing in the sitting room in case anything needed to be done and he'd be listening to all sorts of intimate family conversations – when I became a footman I heard the most outrageous things, but they liked footmen who could look like marble for hours on end.

Buckingham Palace was always slightly behind the times in terms of relationships between servants and their employers. As late as the 1960s there was still a rule that servants cleaned the rooms when the royals were absent, as a former housemaid recalled:

> The family had tea or a glass of water and sometimes a few biscuits in their bedrooms in the morning and each wanted to be woken up at a different time. Only their personal maids and valets were allowed to bring the breakfast tray into the bedroom itself. Then when they came down dressed for breakfast we would go up the servant's stairs – Buckingham Palace has lots of different staircases as you can imagine – to clean the bedrooms and make the beds.
>
> If you happened to see a member of the family in the corridor on your way there or on your way back you had to turn and face the wall. You might be dismissed for looking at them. But the staff regulated these things so well that I'm sure the royals thought their beds got made and their socks were washed by fairies who came in the night. We very rarely bumped into them because the routine was precise and of course they would never use the servants' staircase.

Billy or one of the other footmen would have been responsible for making sure the maids only went to clean the sitting rooms and drawing rooms once they were 'clear'.

After luncheon, most of the servants would have some time off to write letters home in their rooms or they would wash their own clothes or read a book before starting work on dinner. For all servants the rule was one day and one evening off a week.

In many respects servant life was extraordinarily conservative and in ways that seem hilarious today, as another of Billy's contemporaries recalled:

The royals and the people who ran Buckingham Palace had a strange attitude in the 1950s that lasted well into the 1960s, I think. Carpet sweepers and vacuum cleaners were available by this time but many aristocratic families hated change; servants were still cheaper and gave you more status than these labour-saving devices. I once heard a member of a family I worked for say, 'Vacuum cleaners, my dear. They are so dreadfully suburban!' The result was that you would see a line of maids on their knees in the drawing rooms moving slowly across these huge carpets and cleaning them with little brushes and pans as they went. It was ridiculous.

Chapter Seven

A boy at the palace

THERE IS NO question that, right from the start, Billy enjoyed his life in the palace. He was already learning to appreciate the beautiful things with which he found himself surrounded – the palace was, and is, filled with treasures dating back to the time of George III and beyond. Billy quickly developed an eye for good things and in a small way began collecting.

He recalled later: 'I always wanted the finer things in life – or at least I wanted to know about them and mix with people who knew about them. I was first and foremost a collector. I liked to have interesting things around me even as a very young child.'

Throughout his life his friends commented on how impressed everyone was at Billy's instinctive good taste.

Billy's friend Basia Briggs remembers: 'Like many gay men, William just had instinctive good taste. He liked beautiful things and was hugely appreciative of them.'

Roger Booth, a friend from the early days, agreed:

Billy's tiny room at the palace had just his suitcase and some writing paper, pens and pencils and a picture of his family when he first arrived, I seem to recall. But within a few months he had acquired a little watercolour and he'd swapped his jug and basin from something plain to one of the prettier ones. How on earth he did it I don't know.

Billy was also developing his unique style as a storyteller and as his confidence grew his ability to amuse the other servants grew with it, as Roger Booth recalled:

When he wanted to camp it up a bit he was very funny, rather like Kenneth Williams but without such extravagant mannerisms. He had a brilliant way of pausing and making eyes if someone said something that was open to a slightly saucy interpretation. I remember once someone said 'Cook has a problem in her premises', and Billy instantly replied with pursed lips and a knowing glance, 'Mmmm… does she now?' Everyone laughed even though he was later reprimanded for the remark. Billy did this sort of thing automatically. It was part of his personality right from the start. It was his way of being noticed. And he quickly realised that similar quips and funny references to people and things would make people remember him and want to have him around.

Towards the end of 1953 Billy moved from Buckingham Palace, where the young Queen Elizabeth and her husband Philip and young children were now based. He had persuaded the Comptroller of the Household that his first loyalty lay with the Queen Mother, although there is some evidence that the young Queen Elizabeth was keen to see Billy moved on. A former lady in waiting who did not wish to be named said:

> Billy was charming and immensely useful but Elizabeth – the young Queen, I mean – perhaps recognised something slightly wild in him that instinctively made her wary. But she knew her mother was more than a match for the young man and that he in turn was likely to prove terribly loyal.

Billy's reputation for loyalty was partly based on his personality, but also on the fact that he was homosexual. The assumption was that he would have none of the distractions of someone heterosexual, who might eventually want his own family. He also had an enthusiasm for service that was becoming rare as the 1950s wore on and domestic servants – even for the royals – became increasingly hard to find.

By the late 1950s and into the 1960s things had definitely begun to shift and even the grandest families were beginning to be less formal with their staff. Billy sensed this shift and it added to his confidence. Even as a relatively junior footman he was able to make odd little jokes and amusing asides that would have been unthinkable a generation earlier.

'He was brilliant at these little theatrical asides,' recalled Roger Booth. 'And he had a wonderful drawl which always made the Queen Mother smile. He would say "But my dear, they were simply made for each other", and the word "made" would slowly drip off his tongue.'

This kind of theatricality delighted Billy's friends and his employers because it affected almost everything he did. Whether carrying flowers along the corridors or serving at table, whether leading the corgis or just opening doors, he did everything with a kind of exaggerated flourish. There is a famous photograph of Billy with armfuls of flowers smiling at the camera where he looks almost as if he is himself part of a floral display; the centrepiece of a bright and colourful collection.

Of course, when he made the short trip along the Mall from Buckingham Palace to his new home at Clarence House he would have been acutely aware of how the hierarchy worked both for servants – chambermaids at the bottom and butlers at the top – and for equerries and other well-born advisers. William was a political animal who knew who he had to impress and who he could ignore; who to flatter and who to avoid.

Robert Fisher, who worked at Buckingham Palace in the mid-1950s, remembered meeting Billy for the first time.

He was very self-assured and though he was still a relatively lowly footman – which was admittedly the start if you wanted to climb the ladder – he always behaved as if he had a far superior role. The Queen Mother noticed him from the start, I think. She began to ask for him more often than she asked for other servants but it was all very odd because it happened gradually without anyone really noticing how or why it was happening. Billy had a way of dealing with her which she liked and which he knew she liked.

Roger Booth is certain that the Queen Mother knew Billy was gay and didn't mind in the least.

I would say she positively welcomed the fact, as there had been a long tradition of homosexual servants at Buckingham Palace and Clarence House. Some commentators have said this was partly because the royals felt that their female children would be safer if the male servants were homosexual, but it almost certainly had far more to do with the fact that homosexual servants were perceived – rightly or wrongly – as having less need for a life outside the palace.

And even though homosexuality was illegal until the mid-1960s, the royals took a very lordly view of that kind of illegality. They had always known homosexual men – in service and in their families – and couldn't really understand what all the fuss was about. It's also nonsense, I think, to say that Queen Elizabeth didn't mind so long as her gay servants were discreet in their affairs. I'd say the opposite was true and she liked the fact that her gay servants were often very indiscreet indeed, but just so long as they didn't go too far. It provided a bit of excitement for her and at no risk to herself or her reputation. She famously said that without gay servants the royal family would be reduced to 'self-service'.

If a footman were caught soliciting in Hyde Park and the story ended up in the papers, he could simply be sacked and the royal household would never be mentioned in the newspapers as the person's employer. There was an automatic instinct almost everywhere to avoid any scandal attaching to the royals, which is a very different picture from the picture we have today where I think often people are keen to embarrass the royals wherever and whenever they possibly can. If a servant happened to get caught in the 1950s or early 1960s, the police might also sometimes discreetly contact the palace and there would be a quiet word in the right ear and the servant would be let off with a warning.

But if Billy was sexually indiscreet, he had an uncanny survival instinct and would only ever go so far. He would never allow a sexual conquest to threaten his position. And there were many liaisons both before and after he started his relationship with his lifelong partner, Reg Wilcox.

THERE WAS TO be an unwelcome break in Billy's royal service before he was able to consolidate his position with the Queen Mother. Billy's life as a junior assistant and footman in the stewards' room at Buckingham Palace was interrupted dramatically after little more than a year when he was called up to do his National Service. He had expressed a desire to continue working for the Queen Mother but everything had to be put on hold. Billy spent two years in the RAF and, remarkably, those years mirrored in many ways his life at the palace. As soon as his commanding officer discovered what Billy had been doing before call up, he asked him 'on the spot, there and then', as Billy himself later recalled, if he would like to do something similar in the air force. Billy felt it would be no bad thing and found himself assigned as batman to a 'rather delicate but aristocratic senior officer'.

It is interesting that, even in the RAF, a very different environment in many ways from the palace, Billy found his natural role as servant to someone from a socially superior background. 'He was a very nice man,' Billy said. 'Very grand, but kind, and I learned a huge amount from him about how to behave.'

Billy was always slightly reluctant to talk about his time in the RAF. To some extent he felt it was two wasted years; years he could and should have spent working for the royals. 'We did have some fun,' he once said, 'but thank heavens I didn't have to play at soldiers for too long!'

It was towards the end of Billy's National Service – two years was then compulsory – that the widowed queen, knowing that Billy had expressed a desire to work for her, arranged for a letter to be sent to him offering him a job at her new home, Clarence House. That's one story. A more likely account is given by Reg Wilcox ,who said Billy wrote several letters to the Queen Mother after the King died to ask if he could come back and work for her.

Reg claimed she remembered him, liked him and said yes. That's all there was to it. If the later story is true it was a repeat of Billy's strategy of always writing directly to the man or woman at the top. After a short stay in Coventry to see his family after he was demobbed, Billy was back in London.

◇ ◇ ◇

*L*IFE AT CLARENCE House was very similar to life at Buckingham Palace: the long days, the hours spent waiting for instructions and endless door opening and serving at table. For years after he started work there Billy lived in a small room at the top of the house, just as he had lived in a small room at the top of Buckingham Palace.

The interior of Clarence House had been largely neglected for more than fifty years. It was threadbare and almost shabby in places. 'It may have been shabby,' recalled one servant, 'but it was definitely shabby genteel. You would find the most expensive objects lying in corners or covered in dust on a forgotten windowsill somewhere.' One of Billy's visitors later recalled the 'rickety old wooden lift', the cold in winter and the general air of decline. But Billy's room was always a little sanctuary of brightness.

It was only when Billy's parents died in the 1970s and he no longer had a home outside the palace that the Queen Mother gave him the use of Gate Lodge, a small cottage just by the entrance to Clarence House from the Mall. Even today the lodge looks like nothing more than a tiny one-storey guardroom, but it was to become Billy's pride and joy and his home for the last thirty years of his time in service.

But for now it was life in a small bed-sitting room.

There is no doubt that from the time he returned to work at Clarence House in 1953 his aim was clear, as he explained in a brief – and slightly drunken – conversation many years later:

> There was something about Elizabeth the Queen Mother that drew people to her. It wasn't just that she had once been queen. It was her personality as much as her status. She inspired respect, even awe, I think. But apart from wanting to work for her I also wanted to get to the top in service. People might have looked down on servants – they certainly still did in the 1950s – but not on the senior servants and certainly not on royal servants. As time passed, of course, and fewer people had servants at all, royal servants came to have an aura of real glamour.

Billy's time as an officer's batman had taught him a great deal about looking after the personal needs of an individual and he made good use of this knowledge. Where other junior footmen would open doors and collect letters to be taken to the post, Billy always went a step further by asking if anything more was required, or he would suggest serving drinks in a certain way, as fellow servant John Hodges remembered:

> Billy had a knack of seeming to anticipate the Queen Mother's needs and in the royal household the family members can tell immediately – or at least they think they can – if someone is prepared to

go the extra mile for them. They recognised loyalty and in their own way they reciprocated where they found it. That's why Billy eventually got his cottage in the Mall. It also explains why, when Billy got into rows with the equerries and advisers, the Queen Mother almost always backed him.

Of course Billy loved praise; he positively bathed in it, but especially when it came from his beloved Queen Mum. But her fondness for him and his habit of constantly suggesting things to her, often in what looked like an over-familiar way, made the equerries and advisers dislike him.

The Queen Mother was a stickler for rules and for doing things properly, but she was quite arbitrary in terms of which rules were to be imposed rigidly and which were to be ignored. Thus, she never forgave her husband's brother for abdicating, yet after she was told that Sir Anthony Blunt, the art historian, had spied for the Russians, she continued to see him, even inviting him regularly to share her box at the opera. She liked Blunt; he was distantly related to her family and had taken tea with her in Bruton Street early in the century. She didn't really care that he had been a traitor. When first told of Blunt's treachery she is reported to have said it was all a long time ago – which it was – and that it was easy to make too much fuss about these things.

But while Billy was opening doors, pouring drinks and helping lay tables, he was also travelling up to Sandringham in Norfolk regularly, as well as to Birkhall on the Balmoral estate in Scotland. He was cementing carefully his relationship with Elizabeth. He was also developing a taste for a very different kind of life from the one he had known as a young man in Coventry.

John Hobsom, who was one of Billy's lovers at about this time, remembered a man driven purely by sex rather than concern for others.

Well, Billy didn't really have lovers, if by that you mean people he might have felt any loyalty to over any period of time. He was loyal to Reg Wilcox in his own way but that didn't include sexual fidelity. Neither of them minded about that sort of thing and in a bizarre way that made them rather like the royals. People at the top of the social tree seem to think it is very suburban and provincial to get all worked up just because one's wife or husband is sleeping with other people.

Billy used to say that worrying about that sort of thing was pointless; he even used the word 'suburban' once, which I thought was a bit rich given that he really did come from the suburbs of Coventry. But I think Billy was right, about sex and the royals, I mean. He was always saying that when he went up to Balmoral or Sandringham the aristocrats and well-born friends of the royals were always bedhopping. I'm pretty sure he was making this up because it was the sort of frivolous, slightly mischievous thing he enjoyed saying, but it didn't mean it was true. He just wanted to amuse and be slightly outrageous; sometimes it was almost as if he just wanted to make a little noise. He didn't like gaps in the conversation! He used to joke that it would be fun to sprinkle flour along the corridors where people slept and then see where the footsteps led in the morning.

And also I think because he was wary of so many of the rather grand advisers he didn't mind saying they got up to all sorts of mischief, but that doesn't mean it was all untrue. He even told me once that he knew a very upper-class drug dealer who used to visit Kensington Palace regularly when Diana, Princess of Wales was alive. But you never knew with Billy where truth ended and a good story began!

One of the Balmoral gillies whose main job was to take the Queen Mother fishing remembered Billy and the Queen Mother and their unique relationship.

The Queen Mother and William were *always* waving and smiling at each other even if they were parting company for only a few minutes – in fact William's mannerisms and whole demeanour become uncannily like the Queen Mother. One of the footmen used to say 'Billy's the Queen Mother in bloody drag!'

The Queen Mother herself would smile at the servants but rarely talk much to them, with the exception of William and her team of gillies, who she knew were much better at fishing than she was and, in the inevitable informality of the river bank, you could end up saying things to her that you'd later regret.

I once said rather irritably 'No, no, no, not like that,' when for the third time she had cast her line to the wrong place. She looked at me and laughed and said, 'Who is the queen? Is it you or me? Oh yes, let me see – it's me, isn't it.' But she was smiling all the while so I didn't think I would be sacked quite yet.

But I don't think the Queen Mother or any other member of the royal family worried in the least about being thought dotty or eccentric.

In fact they enjoyed talking about their own mad relatives. And I think they rather liked Billy, or at least the Queen Mother did, because he was himself rather eccentric.

She used to say, 'Well, of course we're bound to be mad, aren't we, because we spent so many centuries marrying our own relatives.'

Billy loved stories like this but he was careful to re-tell them only to a small group he felt he could trust. He also felt that every intimate story further strengthened his relationship with the Queen Mother. Towards the end of his life, Billy recounted one of his favourites:

The Queen Mother was lunching with other members of the family when she happened to mention Prince Philip's mother, Alice of Battenberg.

Another member of the family responded by saying that Alice was a wonderful person, but was also rather obsessive and that her biggest failing was her insistence that she was having a sexual relationship with both Jesus Christ and the Buddha.

The Queen Mother, to Billy's delight, responded instantly: 'But then Alice always was very spiritual.'

The Queen Mother could also be rather dotty herself, although she was never in the least out of control. In later life this occasionally became more pronounced, particularly when she was in Scotland where she tended to lower her guard. According to one servant she once spent half an hour wandering around the corridors at Balmoral with a long trail of loo paper dangling out of the back of her dress and the servants were all too terrified to say anything. The crisis ended only when one of the footmen ran up behind her and stood on the loose end of the paper.

Billy disliked stories that made the Queen Mother seem ill-tempered or impatient but he didn't mind in the least if they created an image of a woman who was a little eccentric so long as they also suggested her humour, her intelligence or her concern for others. But best of all he liked it when the Queen Mother said something slightly cutting, so long as it was funny. This was true even if the story was at his expense.

A famous story involved Billy and his partner Reg Wilcox arguing over some trivial matter and the Queen Mother, fed up with waiting for Billy, shouting from the top of the stairs, 'When you two old queens have finished, this old queen would like a gin and tonic.'

The story may be apocryphal, but it fits perfectly into what we know of the Queen Mother's ready wit. The part of it that is suspicious is perhaps the reference to 'gin and tonic' because though Billy himself sometimes absentmindedly referred to the Queen Mother's liking for gin mixed with tonic, he knew that she actually only drank gin mixed with Dubonnet, which she often mixed herself.

Billy's trips to Scotland were more or less an annual affair but he never really enjoyed them. 'I only have the corgis for company,' he once said. And he was not always too keen on the corgis. 'I'm going to throw one of them down the aeroplane steps one of these days,' he would sometimes grumble.

Several servants of the time also remember Billy dancing with the Queen Mother at various balls in Scotland. She was particularly fond of Scottish country dancing, as is the Queen, and Billy was frequently invited to join in. On one occasion at Balmoral he was so exhausted from dancing that he went and hid in a corridor. A young Prince Charles hunted him down and said, 'You must come, William; Granny needs you.'

He returned and swept the Queen Mother out across the dance floor before being relieved, ten minutes later, by an equerry who continued to dance with a woman who seemed never to tire. Everyone recalled that she had enormous energy and a great capacity for enjoyment. But she could be cutting if she felt other dancers were not up to her standard. She said to Billy on one occasion, 'Whenever I dance with David [one of the gillies] I have to remind myself to visit my chiropodist.'

Part of the reason for Billy's dislike of Balmoral was that other, local servants tended to overshadow him and partly – and far more importantly from Billy's point of view – Balmoral meant he was trapped in the middle of nowhere. Beyond the gates were miles of open countryside. Compared to the attractions of life outside Clarence House, it was a desert.

Chapter Eight

Life partners

*E*VERYONE SEEMS TO agree that in his youth and well into his middle years Billy was pursued, as one friend put it, 'by sexual demons'. Billy admitted to the same friend that he knew from the day he arrived at Buckingham Palace in 1951 that this was an environment in which he could enjoy himself, because he could tell straight away – using what today would be called his instinctive 'gaydar' – that below stairs the palace was filled with young homosexual men.

John Reynolds worked in the kitchen in the mid-1950s. He recalled his early days with Billy and other servants of the time:

> You felt almost instantly that this was a sort of family – horribly dysfunctional in many ways, but still a family. Most of the men I worked with were delightful and we did have flings with each other now and then and relationships were established.
>
> Two male servants I remember left the palace to live together and do other things – they set up a guest house in the countryside. But Billy was never going to leave – he loved the work in general and the Queen Mother in particular, which is partly why I think he was attracted to Reg Wilcox. Reg was just the same and would rather have died than go and work somewhere else. They were a good example of how gay couples in service could get together – and stay together.

Those who knew both men insist that Reg was very much the passive partner, something that greatly reduced any chance of serious friction between them. But he and Billy also got on well because they had similar backgrounds and because being in service had been central to their lives before they met.

Other similarities between the two men were striking: like Billy, Reg had grown up in the provinces and his parents ran a fish-and-chip shop. Both men had gone into service because they wanted to escape their humdrum lives and be surrounded by glamour and fine things. Both Billy and Reg loved a life that was, by its very nature, camp.

Several of Billy's former colleagues emphasise this camp nature of royal service.

'I don't think you can over-estimate it,' said one.

> You have to remember that the royal palaces and royal life in general, both for the royals themselves and for their servants, are the essence of camp – it is the highest of high camp. All those golden carriages and absurdly pink twin sets, all those rooms full of Russian china and Fabergé eggs. All that theatrical behaviour based on the grand country lifestyle of the Victorian era having survived into the twentieth century in this one little spot in central London. One of Billy's earliest jobs, which he adored, was actually cleaning the Fabergé eggs. How camp is that?!

*R*EG WILCOX WAS born on 4 May 1934 in Wakefield, West Yorkshire where his father ran a fish-and-chip shop in which Reg helped out as a young man. He was called up for National Service in 1951 and served as a private with the King's Royal Hussars. Two years later he applied for a job with the royal family. After a brief interview at Buckingham Palace he became a junior footman in 1954. He was immediately popular and within months everyone – including the equerries and advisers – knew that Reg was someone rather special. He was seen as uncomplaining, extremely efficient, courteous, good humoured and loyal.

By 1957, he was working for the Duke of Windsor, formerly

Edward VIII, in Paris – by all accounts the Duke had asked specially for Reg. In 1959 the Duke's circumstances changed – it is impossible now to find out exactly what happened – and Reg was back in London and working at Clarence House. Some have said that Reg, who was openly gay, had committed an indiscretion in Paris, but it is far more likely the Queen Mother needed someone of Reg's standing and reputation. The Queen Mother's needs would always trump those of the Duke of Windsor.

However, the Duke did pay the young footman a great compliment at the end of their period together, apparently saying that he had never been more beautifully looked after.

There was a short period after Reg returned from Paris when he went back to his father's chip shop in Yorkshire to help out when his mother was ill, but by the late 1950s he was back in London again and firmly ensconced in Clarence House, where he was to remain until his death.

Reg and Billy hit it off almost from day one and they quickly became lovers – though as we have seen it was not for either of them an exclusive sexual relationship. They took holidays together and spent a great deal of their free time drinking and organising dinner parties, especially when the Queen Mother was away and they had not been obliged to go with her.

Even when they went away together for work there was time for relaxing. Photographs of the two men show them at the seaside on a number of occasions and there were also indiscreet evenings of drunken revelry at Clarence House when the Queen Mother was away. A photograph uncovered after Billy's death shows a decidedly drunken-looking Reg wearing one of the Queen Mother's tiaras.

It is ironic that a job that put both men potentially in the public eye also protected them from scrutiny. Once inside Clarence House they could do what they liked, safe in the knowledge that little information about what went on would leak out. Servants gossiping to outsiders were almost always sacked if their indiscretions were uncovered, but both Reg and Billy had grown up at a time when homosexuality was illegal so caution was ingrained. They let themselves go only among friends and with a trusted few at Clarence House.

There were exceptions to this when Billy went 'cottaging' – although so far as anyone can tell they never went looking for men together. Occasionally Reg or Billy – and it was usually Billy – would return from a nocturnal foray looking bruised and battered after a rough encounter with someone who did not appreciate his advances, but he would be patched up and carry on working the next day as if nothing had happened.

The one time Billy needed a more significant amount of time off was after he was stabbed in the leg by a furious young man who he had propositioned when drunk. The wound took more than a week to heal and Billy had to make his excuses and stay in bed. If the Queen Mother suspected anything she did not say and Billy was sent a get-well card and waited on by the lower servants until he had recovered.

After another slightly less damaging encounter, Billy had to pretend that the large plaster on his cheek was the result of a shaving accident – in fact he had been badly scratched by a young man he'd picked up in Soho. When she saw Billy that morning the Queen Mother said, 'I do hope you have not fallen out with one of your young friends. We must ask Reg to keep an eye on you!'

By 1975, Reg had been promoted to Senior Queen's Footman. Then, in 1978, he was promoted to Deputy Steward and Page of the Presence, working directly under Billy. It was a position he retained until his death. Like Billy, he relished his ancient title, however absurd it might sound to outsiders. He was rewarded with the Royal Victorian Medal in 1979 and then a bar to the medal in 1997. The medal had been established by Queen Victoria in 1896 as a reward for personal services to the monarch. Reg was also awarded the Queen's Long and Faithful Service Medal.

Other servants with lives outside royal service were always baffled that Billy and Reg should have suffered decades of low pay without complaint, concentrating instead on these meaningless awards. But, for Billy and Reg, they were not meaningless at all – they gave them the status and sense of self-worth they had always craved.

Chapter Nine

An outsider on the inside

ANY PUBLISHED MEMOIRS of servant life in the early and middle decades of the twentieth century mention aristocratic employers' almost obsessive concern that working-class servants could not be trusted with valuable items. Not only were the working classes seen as congenitally dim, but they were also seen as clumsy, rough and unable to appreciate anything beyond fighting and fish and chips.

Billy and Reg would have been aware of this, but they were famously skilled at looking after the more valuable items at Clarence House. They were taught by the indomitable Walter Taylor and other older servants of the time and, in fact, Billy quickly became something of a connoisseur in his own right.

Former maid Sally Dexter recalled a life that must have been rather similar to Billy's when he first started work. She remembered that 'the mistress had an idea that it would be almost impossible for me not to break everything I touched, so for the first week or so she followed me round the sitting room watching me clean her ornaments. And you know it was ridiculous really because the ornaments were not that delicate, nor were they particularly valuable. She quickly realised I was not a complete clot and after those initial worries she left me alone.'

Billy understood this world but somehow an in-built fastidiousness – a fastidiousness that had shown itself years earlier in his carefully pressed schoolboy trousers and general avoidance of anything dirty or chaotic – made him unusually sensitive to the values of those for whom he worked. An early report by the Comptroller of the Royal Household mentions that William Tallon is 'intelligent, quick to learn and can be trusted with more delicate tasks'.

From 1955 to 1957 Billy's life, to an outsider, might have seemed fairly routine. When the Queen Mother went up to Scotland, to Birkhall, her house on the estate at Balmoral, he accompanied her. His main responsibility – in addition to his customary skill with the gin bottle – was the corgis. And it was Billy who amused Elizabeth by introducing at Birkhall a novel system of getting people to come down for lunch in which he would walk the halls and corridors ringing a bell and swinging a censer like a Catholic priest. He also threw himself into the dances that were a regular feature of life at Balmoral. 'The Queen Mother loved the fact that Billy knew how to enjoy himself. At Balmoral dances the social barriers vanished temporarily and the Queen Mother would frequently ask specifically for Billy if she wanted a partner,' remembered one Balmoral servant. On one occasion Billy excused himself from a dance and found a quiet corner to catch his breath. He had already danced a number of times with the Queen Mother and simply needed a rest.

'Then I heard a high-pitched cry,' he later recalled. 'It was the Queen Mother shouting, "William, William, where on earth are you hiding?"'

When Billy re-appeared looking slightly shame-faced, the Queen Mother would tease him by saying, 'William, I hope you haven't been neglecting me in favour of the young men in the kitchen.'

Occasionally fuelled by excitement and drink Billy would suddenly execute his own version of a Highland sword dance. 'It was very camp, very extravagant and very funny,' recalled a Balmoral gillie. 'It was the sort of thing only Billy could carry off but even so people were worried. I saw people glancing nervously towards the Queen Mother but she smiled and clapped her hands in delight.'

It was at these parties that the royal family could completely relax. One servant recalled HM the Queen, the Queen Mother and Prince Philip at lunch giggling uncontrollably after five minutes of throwing napkins at each other ended when Prince Philip almost fell off his chair.

> They would also do impersonations or silly voices until they were all laughing. Or they would discuss things in the media that had annoyed them. They would always complain in a light-hearted way, but Prince Philip made everyone laugh on one occasion when he said about a journalist who had written about him that he was a 'complete shit'.

At lunch Billy would stand behind the Queen Mother's chair or close by, always ready to fill her glass and those of her guests. Indeed, Billy became famous for making these parties go with a swing both in Scotland and, more importantly, in London. It was famously said of him that if you tried to stop him filling your glass by putting your hand over it he would simply pour the wine through your fingers.

Billy gradually went from opening doors for pretty much anyone senior to him to having doors opened for him by the junior staff once it was realised that the Queen Mother had a special affection for him. All this was entirely unofficial. It was simply that the Queen Mother was gradually coming to rely more and more on this curiously talented young man. She liked him in the early days because he was very funny when he wanted to be, as John Hobsom remembered.

It is a great pity no one made a tape recording of Billy in full flow – I mean in full conversational flow. He could be very funny just in telling a story that might not in itself be funny at all, by which I mean there was no punch line. It was all to do with his delivery, the way he drawled out certain key words, and nothing to do with telling jokes. There was something wonderfully theatrical about his tone, his timing and the gestures he made. I can quite see why the Queen Mother loved having him around. He had an ability to sing for his supper, as it were, that hardly anyone else has ever had.

But he also had a tremendous ability to flounce out in a rage when the need arose. Sometimes he was genuinely cross; at others it was all a pretence. He would do it and the Queen Mother was always amused – so long as he hadn't really lost his temper. She just found him good company and company was what the Queen Mother craved throughout her long life.

Billy could sense when the Queen Mother's luncheon guests had left the room which of them it was safe to ridicule or at least gently mock. He very rarely misjudged it. And her life was usually so serious that she found his attitude delightfully entertaining.

'William, you must tell me what you thought of so and so,' she would say.

Billy would reply by raising his eyebrows, tossing his head a little to one side and saying, 'Well, I'm afraid words simply fail me. Pearls before swine.'

The Queen Mother would throw her head back and laugh out loud.

By contrast, one or two of the advisers and equerries were seen as terrific bores, as one of Billy's closest friends recalled:

> They were loyal, certainly, but often no fun at all. They'd got their jobs
> in the royal palaces because, despite the advantages of birth and edu-
> cation, they were otherwise completely unsuited to any kind of work
> in the modern world. Well, that was what William rather bitchily
> used to say. And they were just too serious.

John Hobsom explained that though the Queen Mother had many duties to fulfil – official duties that is – she also had a tremendous amount of time that could have hung very heavily indeed with-out people like Billy.

> She broke up her long, occasionally dreary days by inviting old friends
> for regular lunches and dinner parties. If she did not have an official
> public engagement she would always invite old friends to Clarence
> House – less so to Birkhall or the Castle of Mey – but above all
> things she detested lunching alone. She avoided it at all costs and in
> truth she didn't much like dining with the other royals either because
> they were not likely to be as amusing as her friends. Films about the
> royals have sometimes shown the family having breakfast or lunch
> together, but this is entirely wrong. It really did not happen that often.

Favoured luncheon guests included many of Elizabeth's contem-poraries – from the days when she first came out, as aristocratic girls still did in the 1920s. Several of these aristocratic friends from her youth had become her ladies in waiting. Very few have ever spoken of their experiences at Clarence House – no doubt with the lesson of Nanny Crawford always before their eyes – but Lady Frances Campbell-Preston, who was a lady in waiting to the Queen Mother from 1965 to 2002, remembered these lunches, and more especially Billy.

She recalled a man who was attentive but occasionally temperamental. He was also very good with the corgis, but it is doubtful he really liked them. He knew he had to be good to them because the Queen Mother and Her Majesty the Queen – but certainly not the younger royals – were devoted to them. Any sign of dislike would not have been welcomed at all. This is why in so many royal photographs Billy can be seen serious-faced and usually rather dashing in the background leading one or two of the little dogs. In one photograph he can be seen carrying a corgi wrapped in a blanket up the stairs of an aeroplane. The Queen Mother never considered flying the corgis to Scotland an extravagance, as Billy himself recalled:

> Well, I did get cross with her sometimes because she had no idea how the rest of the world lived. She would have hired an aeroplane just for the dogs if it had been necessary. She would leave me a letter asking me to arrange for a helicopter to arrive twenty minutes later than planned as she wanted a slightly longer luncheon or something similar. It never occurred to her that it might have been very expensive to keep a helicopter waiting, but on the other hand she was a queen and she had spent her life behaving in a certain way and wasn't going

to change for anyone. That was part of her charm. I don't think she was in the least bit self-conscious in the sense that she never questioned her own behaviour or thought she was either extravagant or privileged. That was her great strength. But it could be bloody irritating. You got a strong sense of her being entirely cut off from the real world in her constant complaints that Clarence House was a dreary, poky little house – she really said that often. She wanted something far bigger. But then she'd grown up in Glamis Castle and had spent her youth travelling between other castles. She was the genuine article if you see what I mean.

Among the royals the Queen Mother was always the least bothered by protocol. Many of the rules that surrounded her were perfectly understandable – guests at her luncheons completely understood why she would be served before anyone else and that lunch would only be over when she decided it was over. But other traditions were positively rejected by the Queen Mother.

There had long been a rule, for example, that when the royal host (or guest) at the head of the table stopped eating everyone else had to stop. The Queen Mother said about this, 'We can't possibly stick to it. I eat so little that my guests would starve if we did.'

And it is certainly true that as she grew older she ate less and less. She amused Billy on one occasion when her food arrived by saying, 'William, I asked for fish and they appear to have cooked a whale for me.'

She had a wonderfully restrained, dry aristocratic wit that revealed that she was in essence a Victorian. She had a Victorian sense of the need for restraint and economy of expression; a sense that it was unseemly to get worked up about anything and that dry wit would always win the day. When student protesters threw loo rolls at her she famously picked one up and handed it back, saying, 'I think this is yours.'

If Billy inadvertently served an unusually small gin at lunch she might say, 'William, do remember that when it comes to gin I have my reputation to consider.' Billy obligingly topped her glass up.

One of Billy's own favourite stories involved the Queen Mother discussing a lunch party with Billy and then during a long pause she said, 'William, I wonder if we might invite Reginald to join us? It will be like St Trinian's!'

Billy was less pleased with a remark the Queen Mother made when he had irritated her by arriving late one morning and then being in a bad mood. She always knew when he was cross because he would say a curt 'Good morning, ma'am', and then fall silent, in contrast to his more usual merry chatter. If he was in a really bad mood he would begin a slightly manic process of appearing to tidy various objects on the tables in the room but he was really just moving things about unnecessarily and making a great deal of noise as he did so, almost like a child trying to attract attention.

According to one version of events, the Queen Mother became increasingly irritated by Billy's sulk, picked up a newspaper, flicked nonchalantly through it for a while and then said, 'William, you might be interested in one of the situations vacant in today's *Times*. Yes, I'm sure it's just right for you. They are advertising two positions in Sydney.' Others have insisted that the Queen Mother would never have said anything quite so vulgar and that the jibe actually came from one of Billy's fellow servants.

Whoever said it, the fact remains that it was a rebuke that, like all amusing comments, would have spread quickly through the household.

It was rare for the Queen Mother to be deliberately cutting to Billy, but it happened more often than people realised. Billy always gave the impression that he and the Queen Mother were always of one mind, which was not entirely true.

The Queen Mother's occasional sharp remarks must have reminded Billy of his own mother, which would explain why he never really took them to heart. And besides he was more than capable of delivering his own put-downs to those who irritated him. Of one gay friend he was overheard to say, 'Oh yes, Gary is a fool and you know what they say – a fool and his morals are soon parted!'

He also occasionally got into a slightly sarcastic sparring match with the Queen Mother and she did not always get the best of it. After a particularly lengthy lunch with some of her oldest friends the Queen Mother said, 'That really did go rather well, don't you think, William? But perhaps we could have a little more gin next time?'

Clearly Billy had not kept her topped up quite as she would have wished. Before he could stop himself Billy snapped back, 'Perhaps we should have it delivered by tanker?'

The Queen Mother took his remark completely in her stride, refusing to acknowledge the sarcasm. She merely said, 'I don't think that will be necessary, William.'

The corgis, a legendary part of royal life, have been written about extensively. Some commentators believe all the royals actually hate them but are terrified to get rid of them in case the tabloid newspapers accuse the family of cruelty to animals.

Brian Hoey, who has written a number of memoirs of life in royal service, recalled that the corgis served at least one useful function – they gave the household servants early warning that the royals were just about to appear because they had a habit of running on ahead.

Both Hoey and various servants of the time recall that the footmen rather disliked the dogs, some of which were bad tempered and inclined to bite. They were also not fully house trained and a supply of soda water and blotting paper had therefore to be kept on hand at all times to mop up an endless series of puddles.

One of Billy's favourite stories concerned the corgis. When the mood took him he liked to exaggerate how badly behaved they were. He explained how one belonging to the Queen came off rather badly in a fight with another dog and had to have her leg amputated. Both her ears were also ripped off. The dog's name was Heather and the Queen brought her along to Clarence House when she was coming for tea.

William and Mr Baker, another footman and one who knew nothing about Heather and her battles, were merrily getting drunk on pink gin in the kitchen and when Mr Baker, in the course of his duties, saw the dog, he went running back to William saying the gin was too strong as he had just seen a three-legged dog with no ears. William would weep with laughter as he told the story.

But if Billy disliked the corgis, he disliked other aspects of the royals' lives even more.

At Birkhall, Billy didn't take to salmon fishing – the Queen Mother's other passion aside from parties – but he occasionally accompanied her to the river to help with picnics and drinks, especially drinks. He was always wary of the gillies, who were greatly liked by the Queen Mother – one or two had been with her for more than twenty years. Her favourite gillie, who did not want to be named, remembered a woman who loved salmon fishing but only if it came with a glass of her favourite tipple and her favourite page. And Billy was as skilled with the gin on the riverbank as he was in the dining room in London.

A T BIRKHALL, SANDRINGHAM, Windsor and Clarence House – and especially when he accompanied her abroad – Billy gradually made himself indispensable.

The exact process by which he did this went unnoticed by the other staff, as Ronald Smith, who worked at Sandringham, recalled.

> Billy just had a knack of doing the right thing at the right time and when he turned on the gay charm, as we used to call it, he was irresistible. He also had a very protective air about him – protective, I mean, of those he liked. Even members of staff who didn't really like

him at all – because he sometimes behaved as if he was too good to talk to the rest of us – would admit that Billy played Elizabeth like a bloody fiddle.

She thought she was running the show but in many ways it was really Billy who was in charge. I don't mean this in the sense that Billy ordered her about as John Brown was reputed to do with Victoria, but in the sense that Billy really was like a drug to Elizabeth. She tried to do without him now and then, especially if she thought he was getting a bit too big for his boots, but she quickly found she missed having him around – she really couldn't do without him. I think so far as it was possible for her, she was a little in love with Billy.

Billy was even-tempered, skilful at assembling guests and making them feel relaxed. He was also very good at getting them in and out of a room – and in and out of Clarence House – discreetly, without bothering the Queen Mother herself and, crucially, without making the guests feel they were being shunted about too much.

It was a rare skill and a skill that numerous guests paid tribute to over the years. But the real Billy was a far less patient figure than his professional life would lead one to imagine, and occasionally it all went wrong, as Ronald Smith explains:

I can remember one luncheon party where Billy was doing his usual thing of greeting the Queen Mother's guests and plying them with drink. There were a couple of serious types at this luncheon who Billy told me later had asked for water or lemonade or something similar. He was very scornful of people who wouldn't drink alcohol because he felt the party would not really get going without a few gins to start followed by wine. So he got them their lemonade and surreptitiously splashed a bit of vodka in each glass so they wouldn't taste anything. The luncheon party went very well and the Queen Mother later told Billy how much she had enjoyed it and that she was surprised how jolly the two teetotallers were. Billy never let on, but the two whose drinks had been spiked wrote to complain at what had been done to them and Billy was reprimanded by one of the equerries. Typically, he took absolutely no notice, and continued his policy of making everyone drink if he possibly could.

On another occasion, when he tried the same trick, one of the Queen Mother's guests – who happened to be an old friend – complained to her that his drink had been tampered with and Billy got a further ticking off. He was in a bad mood that day and when the Queen Mother spoke to him his face became very red and he suddenly – and very rudely – turned on his heel and stormed off without a word.

The Queen Mother was usually indulgent when Billy 'had a fit' as she used to say. One or two of the other servants felt that Billy's tantrums, which were a regular occurrence in the staff room but rare with the Queen Mother herself, had something of the theatrical about them. It was almost as if they too were part of Billy's repertoire; his way of entertaining and entrancing the old Queen. Certainly she was never angered or put out by Billy's tantrums, exclaiming as he stormed off, 'Oh, don't be such a silly Billy,' a line that seemed to amuse her greatly and which she used several times. Billy didn't look back as he flounced off but the Queen Mother was careful never to be too harsh. He had a certain power over her and, in truth, she feared to upset him too much in case he resigned. She really would have felt bereft without him.

From Billy's point of view, his deepening relationship with the Queen Mother made him increasingly aware of his own power. And if power corrupts, it certainly began to corrupt Billy, who felt to some extent that he was invulnerable, especially when it came to the rent boys and other young men he met on his late-night forays to Soho and elsewhere. As one colleague put it, 'Billy began to think he could do as he pleased.'

ALMOST FROM THE time he moved to Clarence House, Billy spent his free time actively pursuing his fellow male servants and bringing back casual pick-ups he met during his free hours late in the evenings and at weekends.

One or two of those who worked with Billy at this time describe him as a sexual predator, but others say that many if not most of the young male servants were happy to take part in what can only be described as orgies.

Brian Wilson (not his real name) describes how he met Billy in a bar in Soho and was dazzled to hear that he worked for the royals. Along with two friends, he was invited back to Clarence House. During the group sex session that followed Billy suggested Brian should sit on the Queen Mother's favourite sofa and there

Billy had sex with him. Brian was convinced that taking risks was part of the sexual thrill for Billy. Another former lover who knew Billy well in the mid-1960s remembered the royal servant's remarkable lack of caution.

Well, William used to hunt alone a lot of the time although even then it was a risky business, but gay men in those days had really sensitive antennae – they had to because if they got it wrong they might easily end up in court, or badly beaten up. Billy just knew when a new member of staff was homosexual – and most, though by no means all, of those who joined the royal household in more menial positions, *were* homosexual. There was a sort of homosexual grapevine outside the palace and mostly around central London and it got around that if you worked at one of the palaces the work was interesting, or at least superficially interesting, and it was also somewhere where you would automatically have a lot of sexual opportunity. You can imagine how word would get around that lots of gay young men were not only working in one place but living there too! They were like bees at a honey pot!

Imagine the servants' quarters at Clarence House with half a dozen or more young randy men all sleeping there every night. And just ten minutes from Soho. I was part of it too and I have to say we had the time of our lives sneaking between bedrooms. Sometimes I'd sneak into a boy's bedroom and there would be another servant there already, and even if they were already having sex they'd invite me to join them, which I usually did. It all made the low pay seem no problem at all! Personally too I have to say that I don't remember Billy coercing anyone – he was good looking in those days and really quite a catch!

Billy took great risks even in his early days at Clarence House probably because, as several of his contemporaries noted, 'he was extremely highly sexed and simply could not stop himself'.

Many of Billy's contemporaries at Clarence House recall that he was a remarkable mix of discretion and recklessness. If he thought he could get away with it he would do it.

Brian Wilson recalled Billy turning up late one evening with a very rough-looking young man who was clearly a drug addict – 'when you know what an addict looks like you never fail to spot one'.

The young man had the sort of skeletal face that goes with long-time addiction, but Billy, who had been drinking, went to great lengths to entertain him. He gave him a tour of the house including a number of the private rooms.

> It was bad enough that he took the young man up to his room for sex, but to have given him a grand tour as well could have led to a major scandal. But I suspect that even though this was relatively early in Billy's career, the Queen Mother would not have sacked him just for bringing that young man in. She just seemed to turn a blind eye to that sort of thing. She also had an instinctive, unshakeable belief in her own power to control events; if she didn't think something bad or embarrassing would happen, then it would not happen.

Perhaps the best example of the Queen Mother's tolerance of her wayward servant occurred when the *News of the World* reported that a 'rent boy' had been invited back to Clarence House by

Billy. The paper made a huge fuss, but the Queen Mother simply responded by saying, 'How kind of William to invite that poor boy in out of the rain.'

Billy seems to have been careful to invite boys back one at a time to Clarence House when the Queen Mother was there, but when she was away he frequently threw caution to the wind and invited two or even three young men at a time specifically because, as one of his contemporaries put it, 'I think he rather had a taste for orgies'.

One or two of Billy's former colleagues and friends believe that Billy's predatory instincts have been exaggerated. They argue that in many cases he simply invited young men back to Clarence House because he wanted to show off, to impress and to entertain.

'He was so proud of his job and his life,' recalled one friend, 'that he always had to have an audience. He would sweep along the corridors explaining in his slightly camp drawl what went on in each part of the house. The idea that he had sex with all the young men he brought back to the house is nonsense.'

When the Queen Mother was away he certainly continued to entertain but not always with the prime aim of seduction. He liked always to have people around him and he didn't mind a bit if other servants gossiped about what he got up to so long as he didn't actually overhear them.

It was the same with boys who stayed the night. The other servants would all know that 'Billy had someone upstairs' and Billy knew they knew, but he just didn't care. After a night of entertaining dubious young men, he would stride along the corridors the next morning 'like the most buttoned-up confidential character you could imagine'. Hiding his hangover, he would check the appearance of each room in the morning with an almost obsessive attention to detail.

It was only later in his career that he took more risks during the daytime, but by then he was at the height of his power.

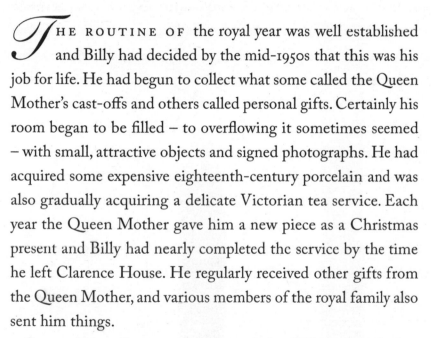

THE ROUTINE OF the royal year was well established and Billy had decided by the mid-1950s that this was his job for life. He had begun to collect what some called the Queen Mother's cast-offs and others called personal gifts. Certainly his room began to be filled – to overflowing it sometimes seemed – with small, attractive objects and signed photographs. He had acquired some expensive eighteenth-century porcelain and was also gradually acquiring a delicate Victorian tea service. Each year the Queen Mother gave him a new piece as a Christmas present and Billy had nearly completed the service by the time he left Clarence House. He regularly received other gifts from the Queen Mother, and various members of the royal family also sent him things.

Some of his colleagues were amazed that Billy accepted what were widely seen among the servants as royal cast-offs. One said:

Part of Billy's job was to go out to Fortnum and Mason and

elsewhere to buy gifts for the Queen Mother's friends, but she never sent out to buy him presents. She just gave him any old odds and ends that happened to be lying about and that she no longer wanted. It was all rather in the manner of Lady Bountiful dispensing charity to the poor, but Billy never seemed to notice or mind.

In fact, Billy delighted in the fact that he was regularly singled out for presents of various kinds. He didn't care that they had not been bought specially for him. He felt that he was being given special treatment, which was hardly surprising given his devotion to the Queen Mother and the fact that, apart from sex, he had no focus at all outside his employment. A colleague remarked perhaps rather unkindly, 'If she had given him a used handkerchief he'd have added it to his collection.'

The 1950s and 1960s were perhaps Billy's happiest time. He was gradually becoming a central figure of importance at Clarence House and with his partner Reg he was able to enjoy a measure of personal domestic life. And Reg never tried to control Billy's sexual promiscuity. He had freedom and security, pleasure and status.

❧ ❧

VARIOUS COMMENTATORS HAVE given different dates for the start of Reg Wilcox's relationship with Billy. By 1960 he had certainly joined the staff at Clarence House, and his route there was remarkably similar to that taken by Billy a decade earlier. Former equerry Major Colin Burgess says that Reg started work at Buckingham Palace in 1954 as a junior footman and then moved to Clarence House in 1960.

Basia Briggs, a close friend of Billy's for more than a decade, thought Reg began working at Clarence House as early as 1957. But, whatever the date, there is no doubt that once they were working together they operated very much as a team. Reg eventually became Deputy Steward and the Queen Mother's Page of the Presence, both titles of course largely meaningless but providing a wonderful echo of the days when well-born children went into royal service. The poet Geoffrey Chaucer, for example, became page – at the age of eight – to one of Edward III's sons (later the Duke of Clarence) in the early 1350s.

Reg was by all accounts very different from Billy. He was always gentle, charming and unflustered. His absolute refusal to lose his temper was legendary. It is difficult to find anyone with a bad word to say about him. But then, he was far less flamboyant and less ambitious than Billy. He was also far less concerned to be close to the centre of the royal family – he had great respect for the Queen Mother but he did not adore her in quite the way Billy did. He was content to remain in the shadow, both of the family and indeed of Billy.

But it was known almost from the outset, and certainly by 1962, that Billy and Reg were an inseparable couple. When Billy died, a signed photograph was found among his possessions. It may have been taken by a member of the royal family and it shows Billy and Reg embracing in the open countryside.

Reg was a calmer, more stable version of Billy and they hit it off from the day they met. Apparently it took Billy just a few days to get Reg into bed. But the relationship developed over a number of years and was definitely about far more than sex.

'They just perfectly suited each other,' recalled one friend.

> They were soulmates if you like. They enjoyed each other's company and in truth I don't think the sexual side of it lasted that long, but the close bond did. They liked to go off to Reg's flat in Kennington at weekends when they could and there they played at being an ordinary couple – having tea in the garden, baking cakes, trimming the roses.

And though Reg was the quiet one, he could let go occasionally. There is a remarkable photograph of him enjoying himself at a party at Clarence House with Billy in which they are dancing together, each wearing one of the Queen Mother's hats.

The Queen Mother certainly knew about their relationship and their exploits and would make occasional quips about it. As William wandered around her sitting room one morning tending the flowers she reportedly said, 'William, I quite understand if you want to wear my hats and other things, but do try to put them back where you found them.'

A number of Billy's friends recall the benign influence Reg had on Billy's character. 'It was a sort of calming influence. Apart from anything else it made him a nicer person,' recalled one. 'He was bitchy far less often and I think the Queen Mother noticed the change. She preferred the slightly mellow version of her favourite servant.'

One of the things that the Queen Mother liked best about Billy was his dry wit and his ability to chatter entertainingly and seemingly endlessly about almost anything. As we have seen, she especially enjoyed it when he mimicked one or other of her more formal friends and others who sometimes came to lunch. But what the Queen Mother probably didn't know was that Billy – and to some extent Reg – also turned their gentle, but slightly mocking laughter on the Queen Mother and the other royals when they had the chance.

Gentle mockery was a good way for servants in general to let off steam, to ease the frustrations of dealing with demanding people who had been trained from birth to consider only their own needs. One of Billy's contemporaries at Clarence House explained:

> Well, if Billy had spent the day running around more than usual for Elizabeth he would sit down with Reg in the afternoon or early evening and start blustering about how difficult the old girl was being. They might imitate her way of asking for things and that would make them laugh and ease the situation. It wasn't done unkindly or at least not when the object of the laughter was the Queen Mother herself.

And this attitude extended to other members of the royal family, especially the Prince of Wales, who was often referred to in private by Billy and Reg as 'she'.

The mockery and laughter might be far harsher if it was directed at one of the equerries or advisers whom Billy really disliked. If Sir Alastair Aird, an equerry who was often uncomfortable with

Billy and Reg, had been talking down to either of them, they would say, 'She's been sticking her oar in and a right bitch she is too. Very hoity-toity, I'm sure.'

The difficulty for Billy and Reg was that they had learned how to dominate and perhaps even cow the other servants, but the senior advisers were a far tougher nut to crack.

Chapter Ten

Feuds and factions

ALASTAIR AIRD (1931–2009) was the
Queen Mother's Private Secretary during
the last decade of her life, but had worked
in the royal household since 1964. Like
many of the grandees employed by the royal family, he disliked
the idea that he should be 'employed' in the sense of being paid.
He had the rather old-fashioned view that gentlemen did not
work for money. It was as if he was afraid people might think his

relationship with the Queen Mother was in any way comparable to that of the other servants. It was part of the gentlemen-and-commons mentality that was, and is, unquestioned in royal service.

Aird's predecessor as Private Secretary, Sir Martin Gilliat, who died in 1993, had been a far more popular figure, even with the overly sensitive Billy.

Indeed, Gilliat was so liked by the Queen Mother that rumour has it he was forbidden by her to retire. Instead, increasingly ill and infirm, he lingered on until the end.

Aird, on the other hand, was respected by the Queen Mother but never much liked; he was perhaps too stuffy and serious a character for a woman who liked her attendants to kick over the traces and leave protocol and decorum behind.

There is no doubt, however, that Aird was as diligent, efficient and just as loyal as Billy. He moved effortlessly from Assistant Private Secretary (where he checked the Queen Mother's arrangements) to Private Secretary, where he double-checked them, as well as looking after travel arrangements, country houses and staffing.

It was no secret that Aird disliked Billy, whom he considered a rather dangerous character who was over-familiar with the Queen Mother, but Aird also had to deal with the Queen Mother's Treasurer, Sir Ralph Anstruther, who, like Gilliat, stayed in post long after a series of strokes had effectively disabled him. Like Gilliat, Anstruther stayed on simply because the Queen Mother hated the idea of him retiring.

So, for many years the Queen Mother's life was run by two eccentric men – Anstruther and Aird – who found it difficult to agree on anything. For a time they refused even to speak to each other. Eventually the situation became impossible and Anstruther was eased out, despite the Queen Mother's objections. It is said that Anstruther cursed Aird as the former left for his ancestral home in Scotland.

The clutter of what Billy sometimes referred to as the 'old buffers' being made to stay on was hardly ideal. No sooner had Anstruther finally retired than Royal Press Secretary Sir John Griffin suffered a series of strokes. And while all this was going on Aird briefed continually against Billy in a desperate attempt to get him sacked. But the Queen Mother would not hear of it. The situation echoes attempts by Queen Victoria's equerries a century earlier to persuade her to dismiss John Brown. Like the Queen Mother, Victoria refused.

In response to hints that Billy really was a bit of a liability, the Queen Mother would say, 'Oh I really think he is quite harmless, and where would poor Reginald be without his dancing partner?'

Aird had been a temporary equerry when he arrived at Clarence House in 1964. After his stints as Assistant Private Secretary he finally became Comptroller in 1974. If Aird was humourless and curmudgeonly he was at least extremely protective of the Queen Mother. He hated the constant press enquiries during her last years – 'What do the guttersnipes want now?' he would ask – but struggled on despite ill health and was still bringing her news during the last week of her life. He later assisted in the arrangements for her funeral.

Aird, who married one of Princess Elizabeth's ladies in waiting, had no experience at all of the real world and thought servants and press people were absolutely beneath him. His biggest problem – and it was a problem that afflicted many of the equerries and private secretaries with a military background – was that he was always sure he was right. If the other advisers and equerries disagreed with him it was simply because they were too stupid to see what he plainly could.

But, ironically, it may well have been his long years working in Clarence House that cost him his life. His former apartment at St James's Palace had been lined with asbestos and he personally supervised its removal without bothering to wear protective clothing. It was soon after this that his health began to deteriorate.

Billy and his partner Reg disliked Ralph Anstruther largely because he had a terrible habit of picking people up on the way their ties were tied or their shoes were polished. It was somehow typical of a world cut off from reality and controlled by people who would have preferred to live in Victorian or Edwardian times.

The wonderfully named Major Sir Ralph Anstruther of that Ilk, 7th Baronet of Balcaskie and 12th Baronet of Anstruther, was Treasurer to the Queen Mother from 1961 to 1998.

Born in London in 1921, Anstruther succeeded his grandfather, the 6th Baronet of Balcaskie, at the age of thirteen following the death of his father when Ralph was just a month old.

In addition to his baronetcy, created in 1694, Anstruther inherited the title Hereditary Carver to the Sovereign and when, in 1980, his cousin Sir Windham Carmichael-Anstruther, 11th Baronet of Anstruther, died, Ralph became a double baronet. 'He was so burdened with titles that Clarence House was probably the only place that would have him,' joked one former junior footman.

Anstruther was part of a small group of ex-army old Etonians who ran the royal household after the death of George VI. For reasons that baffle outsiders, the royal family only ever seem to appoint upper-class men to these positions.

Anstruther's official duties ranged from administering the financial affairs of Clarence House to laying the Queen Mother's wreath at the Cenotaph on Remembrance Sunday and organising the Queen Mother's private holidays each year in France and Italy. Anstruther's perception of the royal sensitivities could lead to delightful absurdities.

For example, the Queen Mother regularly stayed at Maurice Hennessy's estate near Cognac in France and during the 1980s dispute between England and France over lamb exports, Anstruther went to Cognac two weeks before the Queen Mother was due to arrive to make sure that every single sheep she might conceivably lay eyes on had been removed. He also made sure a plentiful supply of the Queen Mother's favourite Tanqueray gin was sent on to Cognac ahead of her arrival. 'Billy poured the gin and Anstruther delivered it on time,' was how one contemporary remembered it.

After Eton and Cambridge, Anstruther had been commissioned in the Coldstream Guards. He fought in Italy and north Africa and was awarded the Military Cross. His army career continued in Malaya where, in 1948, he was saved from drowning by one of his soldiers. After leaving the army in 1959, Anstruther joined Clarence House as equerry and Assistant Private Secretary under

Sir Martin Gilliat. Two years later he was appointed Treasurer to the Queen Mother. He was, among other things, responsible for his employer's private finances and the funding of her household, but appears to have seen his role as keeping Coutts, the Queen Mother's bankers, happy, while allowing the Queen Mother to spend whatever she wanted to spend.

But, if Anstruther saw the Queen Mother as beyond reproach or criticism, which he certainly did, he could be highly critical of the domestic staff – which is where he came into conflict with Billy. Many of their run-ins had more to do with petty rows over precedence and tone rather than anything of real substance. Anstruther felt that Billy treated him with a lack of respect and Billy felt Anstruther was always trying to tell him what to do. Both men knew that Billy was likely to win any dispute by getting the Queen Mother on his side, to the intense irritation of the older man.

Despite their disagreements, even Billy would have accepted that Anstruther could occasionally be a more human character than some of the other advisers. Anstruther was also, and more frequently, delightfully eccentric. He was often spotted in Piccadilly carrying shopping baskets piled high with jars of instant coffee – he was bulk buying for the royal household in person to save money. He also arranged for the Queen Mother to stay at the houses of his grand friends in an attempt to reduce the cost to her finances, which, by the 1990s, were in a parlous state.

Like Billy, Anstruther accompanied the Queen Mother all over the world – on one memorable trip to Italy he stepped out of a

Rolls-Royce in a heavy three-piece suit with rolled umbrella. The temperature was approaching 40 degrees centigrade.

Whatever his eccentricities, however, Anstruther was popular with the Queen Mother because he was from precisely the same social class. If she had a castle in Scotland, then so did he. She was his annual guest at Watten Mains, his shooting lodge in Caithness, and at Balcaskie, his castle overlooking the Firth of Forth. With her love of all things Scottish, the Queen Mother enjoyed enormously her visits to Anstruther's ancestral home, especially as dinners at Balcaskie were always accompanied by Anstruther's personal piper.

Anstruther was also immensely wealthy and is rumoured to have helped the Queen Mother financially on a number of occasions. His London house was on Pratt Walk, a short street of pretty Georgian houses that the Queen Mother was so concerned would be demolished, she is rumoured to have persuaded Anstruther to buy every single house on the street.

Though Billy sometimes disliked Anstruther's fussy ways, other members of staff found him charming. This was partly because he was an unassuming and rather paternalistic man who liked to wander into the kitchens and sometimes even help with the cooking. It was common knowledge in the kitchens at Clarence House that he was an enthusiastic and skilful jam maker, who, when he stayed at his house on Pratt Walk, lived almost entirely on tinned baked beans. Word also got around about the extraordinarily considerate way he treated his elderly housekeeper at Balcaskie.

Margaret had been with him since he was a child and during

her last years she remained in the kitchen, nominally in charge and still able to prepare the food, but too infirm to serve dinner to his guests. Anstruther hated the idea of upsetting her by disturbing her routine, so when his guests were seated at the table he would shout 'We are ready, Margaret,' and then he would leap out of his chair, dash into the kitchen, put the food on the plates and carry it in to his guests. At the end of the meal he would shout 'Thank you, Margaret,' before leaping up once again and clearing the table himself.

～ ∽

*I*F BILLY HAD mixed feelings about Anstruther, Aird and the other advisers and equerries, his admiration for Prince Charles was unqualified. Charles always made a point of talking to Billy, and he had long ago given Billy a signed photograph of himself. Billy also had a specially inscribed photograph of Charles and Diana. He had been particularly close to Diana, who liked the fact that Billy could combine deference and loyalty with an impish sense of fun.

'She loved his funny stories,' recalled one friend of Diana's, 'especially if they involved gentle mockery of the firm.'

> I don't think she liked the rigidity of royal life even before she became part of it. She wanted to have fun and the royals, or at least most of them, simply don't do fun. They take life very seriously indeed and Diana thought this was a very narrow view of life

130

– she wanted life in the round; she didn't mind being serious some of the time or when some public engagement or other demanded it, but in private she wanted to be very different. This was frowned upon by the key members of the royal family and it partly explains why she began to talk to the newspapers and the media in general about her life and its difficulties. I think the sense that she could do this and get away with it came originally from her long intimate conversations with Billy. You can tell that she took to him from their first meeting – which was a good while before she married Charles – because on the night before her marriage she spent a long time cycling around William's office on a small bicycle while he was trying to work and all the while she kept up a long conversation with him.

William liked both Charles and Diana but worried from the outset that they would not make a go of their marriage. 'Utterly, utterly different from each other,' he would later say, but he was a staunch defender of Diana, who he teasingly liked to point out was just as well born as Charles, who was descended to a large extent from minor German princes, whereas the Spencers had intermarried for centuries exclusively with the English nobility.

But, despite their affection and respect for Charles, Billy and Reg couldn't help laughing at some of his enthusiasms, his 'Queenly ways' as they put it. Stories about Charles talking to plants, for example, made them hoot with laughter, though they only ever partly believed them. Reg would run through Charles's more extravagant habits using his favourite epithet.

> Well, she employs 133 staff to cook, clean, tweak and mop up. She needs
> at least sixty domestics: cooks, a head chef, teams of footmen (jun-
> ior and senior), chauffeurs, housemaids, gardeners, cleaners and three
> valets to sort out toothpaste, pants, pyjamas and hot-water bottles.

Billy's mockery of Charles was always gentle because he genuinely liked him, but he was aware that Charles and Diana (and later Camilla) lived a rather cosseted life. Billy insisted, for example, that Charles and Camilla's clothing was never put in a washing machine – the royal couple, according to Billy, were adamant their clothes should be washed by hand.

Billy was once asked if it was true that Charles's shoelaces were really ironed: 'Of course, my dear,' he replied, 'he can't be seen to be slumming it!'

Billy always liked Charles because he was diffident; he was and is naturally inclined to kindness and dislikes excessive formality. Only one royal consistently irritated Billy and the other staff, and that was Edward, the Queen's youngest child. Billy thought Edward insisted on rigid formality among his servants because he was so far down the royal pecking order that his only option was to stand on his dignity.

A number of former royal servants have confirmed that, apart from the Queen Mother when she was alive, the most popular member of the royal family is Prince Philip.

'Oh yes, he is no trouble at all,' said one. 'Very unassuming and knows that it is not always as easy to do something as it is to ask for it to be done.'

Billy's service with the royals occasionally extended well beyond working for the Queen Mother. He might be seconded, as it were, to assist visitors and guests of the royal family. He was particularly proud of a signed photograph given to him by the Duke and Duchess of Windsor, for whom he worked on a number of occasions. He had helped look after the couple on one of their rare, awkward visits to England following the abdication. As the Queen Mother disliked seeing them, Billy had walked a careful tightrope on these occasions and it is testament to his diplomatic skills that he was sent a thank-you gift by a couple who were decidedly unwelcome at Clarence House.

BILLY CONTINUED TO enjoy the attentions and gratitude of various members of the royal family and he was now mixing with theatre people, including the dancer and choreographer Anton Dolin. He never entirely forgot his origins, however, and if old acquaintances from Coventry came to London, which occasionally happened as late as the early 1990s, he would still give them a tour of Clarence House – provided the Queen Mother was away.

Some of these visitors admitted that they had hardly known Billy in his Coventry days but since Billy had become something of a celebrity in the city, many people used the fact that they were at the same school or had lived close by as sufficient reason to claim an acquaintance. They would turn up at Clarence House and just hope for the best and Billy, who loved his claim to fame, never turned them away. He was incredibly proud of working at Clarence House, as one visitor remembered:

> It was as if he had become a pop star. We were in awe both of him and his grand manner and the house. When we got back to Coventry, a visit to Clarence House was something to boast about for the next ten years. But what we marvelled at most was the change in Billy's accent, his manners and his whole demeanour – he sounded as aristocratic as the royals or their equerries!

Barry Fox was Billy's favourite hairdresser back home in Coventry. Whenever he visited his mother he would pop in for a quick trim and regale Barry with tales of life in the palace. Billy was always very generous with his invitations, too. Barry recalled Billy insisting that if he was ever in London he should come straight to Clarence House and there was no need to make an appointment. A few weeks later Barry was in London and decided to take Billy up on his invitation. He arrived at Clarence House and was whisked into Billy's office and then on a lightning tour of the house, which included a great deal of alcohol. Billy seemed entirely in command of the police at the gate, the other servants and even the equerries.

Reta Michael, whose friendship with Billy dated back many years, remembered being shown around Clarence House while the Queen Mother was away.

Reta recalled Billy telling her to wave out the window to a

passing group of tourists. 'They'll never know you're not a royal,' he apparently said to her. 'It will make their holiday to think that someone at Clarence House waved to them.'

Billy's brother-in-law, Frank Oliver, a retired Coventry watch-maker, visited Billy on a number of occasions and each time he recalled the welcome was as warm as ever. Frank was escorted up to Billy's rooms by a policeman who seemed greatly in awe of the immensely self-assured steward. Frank remembered that Billy was enormously proud of the fact that he had been around the world with the Queen Mother. But he used to insist that, while he loved his job and would not change it for any other, it was not all easy going.

On foreign trips he would get to see very little of the country they were staying in – though several of his friends insisted Billy had absolutely no interest in foreign countries anyway, so this was no great loss. However, abroad even more than at home he had to be constantly on call – a job that took up *most* of his time at home took up *all* his time during these trips.

Frank Oliver said that he became such a regular at Clarence House that, on one occasion, the policeman, who was by this time well acquainted with him, gave Frank permission to go up to Billy's quarters alone. Normally he would have been escorted, as would every visitor, but Frank somehow got lost in the big, ram-bling, unfamiliar house. Eventually he bumped into a maid but was astonished at how long he was able to wander at will with-out being challenged.

When Billy's sister Jennie died in 1973 from an asthma-related illness, Frank re-married and lost touch with Billy, but there was always a hope that Billy might visit Frank back in Coventry. He was, after all, godfather to Frank and Jennie's daughter, Stella.

When he reached the top floor of the house Billy was there to meet him. In his characteristic drawl he said to his visitor, 'Thank heavens it's you. For one dreadful moment I thought it might have been one of my lovers.'

A friend of Billy's who didn't wish to be named, noticed immediately that rubbing shoulders for so long with the royals, especially the Queen Mother, had given Billy a sort of 'London polish' that had left only a few traces of Coventry. Billy had almost completely lost his accent and he had a kind of careful, aristocratic way of moving and talking.

'I remembered that he had always been a good mimic and very observant,' recalled his friend. 'Having worked for the royals for so long Billy had unconsciously become rather like them. At one point and rather maliciously I thought he even had some of the Queen Mother's mannerisms.'

All Billy's old friends from Coventry who made the trip to London treated Billy as if he had become a film star. Billy himself knew that whenever he appeared in later years in photographs standing behind the Queen Mother, the picture was bound to be re-printed in the Coventry newspapers. It was why he so carefully manoeuvred himself into the camera shot on so many occasions and it was why the Queen Mother reportedly once said to him at the beginning of one of her birthday walkabouts, 'Come along, William. Your public is waiting for you.'

But Billy's few remaining Coventry contacts knew that the ties to his home had really been broken. One friend recalled that shortly before he left to catch the train home, he was offered tea in some 'absurdly delicate little cups'. Billy asked about various people they had both known, but 'we were so different now that I knew as he escorted me down and out of the house that I would probably never see him again, and of course I didn't'.

Chapter Eleven

Wine and roses

A TYPICAL DAY FOR Billy would start at around six in the morning, at which point he would spend at least half an hour carefully dressing in his white tie and tails. He always claimed he much preferred this get-up to the tight tunic with brass buttons up to the neck that he had to wear as a junior footman.

White tie and tails from early morning 'til late at night would have irritated a lesser man, but Billy enjoyed the uniform almost as much as the job. Indeed, he hated to be seen in anything else while he was at work.

Towards the end of the Queen Mother's life, whenever he went out he would leave instructions that he should be telephoned immediately if there was any news about the Queen Mother's health. On several occasions this happened and he was soon after seen running across the grounds from Gate Lodge desperately trying to put his shirt and tie on while simultaneously combing his hair.

'He was a terrific dandy,' recalled one friend. 'He absolutely loved dressing up, but especially as the royal household had him measured for all his suits – they were handmade and would have been completely beyond anything Billy could afford if he had not been in royal service.'

After dressing, Billy would visit the kitchens where the Queen Mother's breakfast had been prepared. This was invariably tea and biscuits or tea and a bowl of seeds. Billy would enter at precisely the same time each day and hover. 'He was a great hoverer,' recalled one of the maids.

Immaculately dressed as ever, Billy would pick up the tray, inspect it with a very serious look on his face and then stalk off like an elegant if rather gloomy heron, leaving the kitchen door to swing shut behind him. He would carry the tray to the Queen Mother's apartments and leave it on a small table outside her bedroom.

It has been said that he was the only male servant allowed into her bedroom without knocking but this was almost certainly something Billy himself put about. Other servants of the time pour scorn on the idea.

> She had her own personal maid who helped her in the morning and it was she who took the tray in. There is absolutely no way Billy would have dared go into her bedroom unannounced. He did sometimes over-step the mark but that would have been too much, even for him.

Former royal servant Liam Cullen-Brooks, who worked closely with Billy, agrees that Billy's intimacy with the Queen Mother was sometimes exaggerated. He insists that her breakfast tray was left outside the bedroom and the Queen Mother's personal maid waited until Billy had departed and only then knocked and took the tray in.

Billy would then spend the morning worrying about the luncheon party that almost always followed breakfast and the long process of the Queen Mother getting ready for her day. She was helped to dress by her maid and would then enter her private sitting room, where Billy would soon appear.

He might be asked to bring the corgis, of which the Queen Mother seems to have been particularly fond, but she didn't pet them much – she simply liked to have them around.

The Queen Mother disliked bad news or anything gloomy, so on most days Billy would put on one of her favourite George Gershwin records, which she might then insist on playing over and over again. She told Billy that the happiest period of her life had been her twenties, which of course coincided with the 1920s, the great era of jazz and, above all, Gershwin.

Billy understood that every generation falls in love forever with the music of its youth, particularly when that music is popular music, and, for the Queen Mother, the music of her youth was, especially, Porgy and Bess. Billy knew a remarkable amount about the Queen Mother's early years because on quiet days she talked to him for hours on end about her distant memories. Billy was astonished when she recalled dancing in the great palaces of Park Lane and Mayfair, palaces demolished as long ago as the 1930s.

> We danced at Holland House in Kensington when the grounds were still a private park and there were at least a dozen grand houses in the West End where we also danced, and it was always a band, not a dreadful gramophone. Indeed we hated gramophones. They were a travesty. Then suddenly the music was gone and the palaces were demolished and turned into flats or converted to offices.

'She complained bitterly', recalled Billy, 'that land taxes and death duties had destroyed the older, wonderful world she had known in the 1920s.' Gershwin and other music of that time was the Queen Mother's route back into an earlier glamorous world.

Even Billy was sometimes shocked at the extent to which the Queen Mother would open up to him on days when there were no engagements and she was, frankly, bored.

She told me she was always astonished that the press thought the royal family never relaxed and spoke to each other in a normal way and never had any fun. In fact, they had huge amounts of fun in Scotland away from the prying eyes of the press. Even Elizabeth and Prince Philip would chase each other and their children along the corridors when they were younger.

The Queen Mother loved to explain how her children had enjoyed playing pranks on her, especially Princess Margaret, who was always hiding things and getting up to mischief. Margaret had once climbed out of a window high up at the front of Clarence House and had to be coaxed down without alarming her – had she realised the danger she was in she might have fallen. Princess Elizabeth, on the other hand, had been devoted to horses and shooting and the Queen Mother worried that the press would get hold of the story that the Queen loved nothing more during the season than picking up at her shoot in the grounds of Windsor Castle. She would say, 'The problem is that as a picker-up she has occasionally to despatch a wounded pheasant and one can't help thinking the press simply wouldn't understand.'

The Queen Mother also thought that it was a terrible mistake that everyone had made such a fuss over Princess Margaret wanting to marry Group Captain Townsend. She thought that if they had been allowed to marry her younger daughter's life might have been much happier.

Billy, however, disliked the way the press increasingly portrayed Margaret as prone to gloom and depression. In fact, according to

Billy, for much of the time she enjoyed her life and, like her mother, relished parties, games and laughter. One of Billy's favourite stories described how he happened to be walking along the corridor outside the Queen Mother's private apartments when he heard a crash. He carefully knocked and entered to discover the Queen Mother and Princess Margaret in fits of giggles because they had inadvertently overturned a tray of drinks. According to Billy this was absolutely typical of the two women – they inspired laughter and fun in each other to the point where something outrageous might easily happen.

She once told him that she often wondered what life would have been like for her if she had never married into the royal family. She thought she might have been able to write books like the Mitfords or do something outrageous or scandalous. Billy claimed that on a number of occasions she had said to him, 'Sometimes one simply wants to do the wrong thing to see what it would be like. Kicking over the traces must be such fun.'

These conversations and others like them took place in the mornings when Billy and the Queen Mother might find themselves together and entirely alone for long periods.

'She liked to talk at these times,' remembered Billy, 'but far more than talk, she liked to dance.'

It was above all things the pastime she pursued with a real passion and as she had few partners who were deemed suitable, I was often drafted in. And she might decide to dance on a whim when one was least expecting it, perhaps five minutes before her luncheon guests were due to start arriving.

She sometimes found the constraints of life in the royal family tedious and would occasionally let go. On one memorable visit to the singer Elton John's house near Windsor Castle, accompanied as ever by Billy, she insisted on dancing with the singer while wearing one of his extraordinary glittering sequined jackets.

But the happiness of the day could easily be spoiled if the preparations had not been made. For example, the sitting room Billy and the Queen Mother shared in the mornings had to be carefully prepared each day or the Queen Mother would be upset, as Billy explained: 'We had to make sure that fresh flowers were ready every morning in bowls and vases in the Queen Mother's sitting room and dining room. They were changed every day because if they were not fresh she immediately noticed. They affected her whole mood.'

By contrast the serious aspects of the outside world were anathema to her. Billy always said that she disliked politics and current affairs because, for her, they were a reminder of the horrors of the War – 'in her case two wars', as Billy liked to point out.

'She hated listening to the news on the wireless or even worse on television,' recalled one of her maids.

> She said it was all too depressing and that one should concentrate only on life's pleasures and ignore unpleasantness of every kind; she thought we should all concentrate on fun and gaiety, but of course that was easy for her and not so easy for the rest of us. I don't think she knew the least thing about current affairs or politics or how ordinary people lived. She simply tried not to worry about what was happening in the outside world.

If she didn't have letters to write – and in truth most of her letters were written on her behalf by her Private Secretary – she might glance at a magazine, hardly ever at a newspaper. Many people thought she read magazines such as *Country Life* and *The Field*, but Billy insisted she wasn't that keen on either. One of her favourite magazines, apparently, was a curious little publication that came out quarterly and actually looked far more like a book than a magazine. It was called *The Countryman* and was published from an old house in Burford in Oxfordshire. It concerned itself with rural history and archaeology, with articles about odd characters, eccentric churches and long-forgotten traditions.

'I think she liked it because it avoided all the *nouveau riche*, rather vulgar material to be found in other magazines,' said Billy.

Sometimes, despite their intimate conversations, the morning would drag and Billy would know that it was up to him to provide the entertainment.

'Where the Queen Mother was concerned,' recalled a junior butler who worked closely with Billy for a number of years, 'Billy was a wonderful conversationalist. It's very hard to catch his tone and his style but it was a mixture of drawl and wit, slightly bitchy and often very funny, but in a way that suggested he wasn't really trying to be funny.'

The Queen Mother was always very particular about who she invited to lunch, but occasionally she would feel she was compelled by circumstances to invite someone unlikely to sing for his or her supper. She would say, 'Oh dear, so and so is coming to luncheon. What shall we do with him? William, will you give him a chair with a view out the window? He will be so much happier not having to bother much with the rest of us.' Or she would say, 'William, I fear luncheon today may be rather a trial.' Billy would nod sagely and assume that this was an indication that he would need to make an extra effort with the guests.

'Much of what they said to each other was really in a sort of code,' recalled a contemporary. 'The Queen Mother might make what to the rest of us would seem like a bit of small talk, but Billy often knew that she was asking for a slight change in the way things were to be organised on that particular day. He was very sensitive to that sort of thing.'

On other days the Queen Mother would 'potter quietly' until she felt it was time for her first gin, which she might have at around eleven o'clock. But throughout the morning and always ready with the gin and the conversation, Billy would wait quietly and unobtrusively in the background. If she got up, he was there to open the door and close it behind her. It was a level of personal attendance that is almost incomprehensible to those who have not seen it at first hand.

'If she needed something he was there ready to run and fetch it,' recalled another former colleague.

She rarely lifted a finger to help herself even in the 1970s and 1980s when she was perfectly healthy. If she wanted the window to be opened she would ask Billy to do it; if she wanted a book from a side table three feet away she would ask Billy to bring it. She almost never opened a door herself. I think she knew that other people didn't live the way she lived but it would have been very difficult for her to imagine what it would really be like to live without servants, since she had never done it herself. She might have been a patron of many charities but, like all the royals, it was seen very much as just part of what the royal family did. Her world was the only world she had known. She was as trapped in it as any of those who worked for her. More so, in fact, as they could leave. And whatever else one may say about her, it has to be admitted that she was always determined to do what she felt she had to do. She wanted to behave as she felt the Queen Mother should behave.

Billy had some of the same feeling. He felt it was important that he should do his duty even if this often meant waiting and trying, so far as possible, to anticipate the Queen Mother's needs.

In later years when he was a little disillusioned with life – this was long after the Queen Mother's death – Billy would sometimes say, almost under his breath, 'I spent most of my life standing around waiting.' Though he was delighted when, to cheer him up, a friend quoted to him the last line of Milton's poem 'On His Blindness': 'They also serve who only stand and wait.'

Despite the long hours and long periods spent waiting, Billy enjoyed the feeling that at any time, day or night, he might be needed.

After breakfast, then Billy, then an early gin, the Queen Mother might have a morning meeting with her equerry, Sir Alastair Aird, or with one or other of her personal advisers, who would brief her about any visits planned for that day or later in the week.

Although, of course, as the years passed and the Queen Mother became increasingly frail, the number of visits and appointments decreased dramatically.

Well before lunch Billy would start what the other servants saw as his 'theatricals'. It is a word that finds an echo in almost everyone's memories of Billy at work, and indeed at play. He was intensely theatrical, a director *manqué*. His stage was Clarence House and his actors the royals, their advisers and friends. Luncheon, being no exception, was a carefully stage-managed theatrical event.

It had to be so, because it was something the Queen Mother loved. 'In many ways – compared at least to the lives of ordinary people – her life was rather empty,' remembered one former footman.

> Her luncheon parties were vital to her good temper – if nothing was planned I think she panicked a little at the prospect of an otherwise empty day stretching ahead of her. If you think about it you can see why – she couldn't go shopping or to the library; couldn't go out for a stroll round the block, or stop at a little café for a cup of coffee. All these ordinary things were entirely closed to her. The lunches were her lifeline.

Curiously, although the food was always very good at these lunches, there was a sense that it was not important, at least not to the Queen Mother. Indeed, the royal family has long had a curious attitude to food, which combines frugality with extravagance in a unique way. It has often been observed that members of the royal family barely touch a thing at official dinners. The Queen Mother ate little at her own luncheons and famously once said she only liked lettuce because she could hide her food underneath it.

Various commentators have noted the royals' passion for eggs and the Queen Mother was no exception. She was particularly fond of a dish known as Oeufs Drumkilbo, a rich mix based on eggs and mayonnaise and named after the next estate along the river from Balmoral. For pudding she enjoyed After Eight ice-cream, an extraordinary concoction involving, among other ingredients, two boxes of After Eight mints and six egg yolks. Another favourite was Soufflé Rothschild, a dish requiring large quantities of eggs and, originally, real gold leaf.

The food, however, was always just a means to an end – it was company and conversation the Queen Mother really relished. As she grew older and lunch parties became a less frequent occurrence she relied increasingly on Billy to amuse her.

She knew that when Billy was in charge, any luncheon party was bound to go well. She expected her guests to entertain her, which is why she hated it if they sat tongue tied and too awkward to begin to talk. If they were amusing, they were sure to be invited again. She must have realised that if her guests were reluctant to speak it was because they were nervous about saying the wrong thing in her presence, but Billy was the solution to all forms of nerves and awkwardness.

He would first check the invitation list to see who was invited to lunch or, less often, dinner, and then work out the best way to place the guests at the table to make them feel comfortable.

Sometimes the Queen Mother would insist that a particular person should sit next to her. When the guests arrived, Billy moved swiftly into action. As one friend remembered, Billy was 'the last word in meeting and greeting'.

After twenty or thirty years in the job, Billy sounded, as we have seen, almost as aristocratic as the Queen Mother herself. He was also immensely confident in his abilities. He employed little tricks to make the guests feel flattered, that their interests or importance had been taken into account. If a Russian princess happened to be on a luncheon list Billy made sure that a genuine Fabergé egg – carefully selected from the royal collection – was placed in front of her place setting. If a painter had been invited, a small sketch from the royal collection might be added to the place setting; for an actor, a rare theatre programme.

According to Billy, careful preparation was absolutely vital if these lunches were to go well. He was under a great deal of pressure in this respect because although she felt he was incomparably good at this sort of thing, the Queen Mother would be cross – and would certainly blame Billy – if things did not go well.

Once the table was ready and the room had been filled with vases of flowers, Billy would prepare to meet the guests in the hall where they entered Clarence House before escorting them to the dining room.

Once in the dining room the guests might be surprised to discover that the Queen Mother was absent. She always waited until Billy had dispensed a few drinks before entering – members of the royal family always arrive last and leave first.

Billy was always very careful with the drinks. The wine cellar at Clarence House was very much his domain, and over the years he learned a great deal about both it and its contents. He made sure that the royal household drank only the finest wines and they were ordered from Britain's oldest wine importer – Berry Bros & Rudd in nearby St James's. The firm, which has been trading from the same premises since the late seventeenth century, is run today by the eighth generation of the same family. Anyone who has visited the shop will immediately appreciate how and why it delighted Billy. The shop fittings appear to have been unchanged for centuries and the assistants have an air of patrician gravitas more in keeping with the sellers of expensive pictures or antiques.

Armed with numerous bottles of irresistible wine, as well as the Queen Mother's favourite Tanqueray gin and Dubonnet, Billy then poured and encouraged, encouraged and poured. We've seen how he occasionally spiked someone's drink but Billy had another tactic when someone asked for water or a non-alcoholic drink. He would gravely incline his head, turn on his heel and then ignore the request unless it was repeated – several times.

One guest recalled asking for water and being given an almost savage look by Billy, who responded by giving him a glass of water *and* a glass of wine. Later during lunch itself this particular guest noticed that his glass of water was quickly removed by Billy, even though he had hardly touched it, and meanwhile his wine glass was carefully re-filled even after the tiniest sip.

When the Queen Mother finally entered – Billy having magnificently opened the relevant door – everyone would be 'significantly under the influence', as one lunch guest recalled. With the Queen Mother seated, conversation – rather subdued and over-cautious – would begin.

Inevitably the Queen Mother was obliged by the rules of etiquette to say something relatively bland. 'She really did ask me if I had come far,' recalled one luncheon guest. But precisely because she had to make trite comments, she hated it if her guests responded too much in kind. She was once asked by a luncheon guest how old the corgis were. She could barely supply a civil answer and complained bitterly that she had been 'reduced to discussing the age of the dogs'.

Billy knew that the only way to get the Queen Mother's guests to really relax and talk in the light-hearted way they would talk at any other party – which is what the Queen Mother really wanted – was to make them tipsy, hence his legendary manipulation of the bottle.

Despite Billy's attempts to control all aspects of the Queen Mother's social schedule, there were times when events got away from even him. On one widely publicised occasion after lunch he had to stand and bite his lip while a TV presenter, the late Desmond Wilcox, pushed a microphone into the Queen Mother's face and asked a series of questions for which she had been given no warning. It was a huge breach of etiquette and would have left Billy incensed, but he knew it was not his place to intervene. The nightmare ended when the Queen Mother simply smiled, turned on her heel and left the room – without answering Wilcox's questions.

And if there happened to be no lunch on a particular day her consumption of gin might increase significantly, but she was never out of control. She liked to be relatively sober at her luncheon parties because she enjoyed seeing her guests become less inhibited as they gradually became more inebriated. Since she drank pretty much the same amount every day – 'throughout her life she drank almost continually,' recalled one adviser – she knew precisely how much to drink to make sure she was always slightly less inebriated than her guests.

'We got to the stage', one guest remembered, 'at which we were vying with each other to say increasingly risqué things that might amuse the Queen Mother. Every bit of the table's conversation was directed at her even though we vaguely pretended at times that we were really talking to each other.'

I remember saying about a well-known actor that he was a complete arse and then freezing in horror for perhaps half a second. But then I noticed the Queen Mother was smiling broadly and she said, 'Did you say complete?' The whole table was visibly delighted – and probably relieved that I hadn't been chucked out on my ear.

It was like a medieval court where we competed to be witty so she would hear and approve and perhaps invite us again. We knew that bores were never given a second chance. So a very odd atmosphere prevailed that was slightly artificial. It may have been different for others, I don't know, but for me it seemed very eccentric. The Queen Mother herself said very little – the result of a lifetime's habit of reticence, I think – but she felt she was part of something more relaxed, more expansive, if people around her did what she could not easily do herself and told funny, even ribald stories.

Another guest, one of a long line of painters, commissioned at various times to produce the Queen Mother's portrait, explained how she liked these parties to go:

She wanted above all to be entertained and to escape for a while the restrictions that are inevitable if you are a very prominent member of the royal family. I remember telling a story that I would not have dared to tell if I had been sober. I was telling my neighbour, but as I was placed just two from the Queen Mother herself I knew she would be listening.

I was explaining that an old Etonian friend of mine, who was a very senior director of an old banking firm in the City – a banking firm that still retained many of the traditions of its seventeenth-century founders – had told me how, one night, he had had to return to the office to collect some papers he had forgotten and needed to work on at the weekend. Having reached his floor – and remember this was a bank – he found a large, very tough-looking skinhead asleep on the floor behind his desk. He was about to call security when in a moment of madness he decided to deal with the situation himself. He prodded the sleeping skinhead, who was wearing huge vicious-looking boots and was covered in tattoos. The young tough woke up and in order to cow him the banker asked what the hell he thought he was doing. He followed this with a string of expletives and was astonished when, in a highly educated voice, the skinhead replied,

'How dare you speak to me in that fashion. There is no need to use such foul language.' He then hopped up on to the window ledge, opened the window and disappeared across the rooftops. The Queen Mother was delighted by this story and seemed disappointed that I was unable to tell her more. But that's how she saw her lunches: they were a way to get people to talk about the real world outside her gilded cage.

At a pre-arranged and very subtle signal, the Queen Mother would indicate that luncheon was over. Billy would appear behind her chair, easing it out from under her. She would stand up and move towards the door where Billy would already be waiting to open it. The Queen Mother would wave airily and tell everyone to carry on as long as they liked. Billy would see her out of the room before returning to ensure the guests were given a short time to collect their thoughts (and their things) before being politely told it was time to go. They would then be escorted out of the building.

Having supervised the clearing of the table and restored order to the dining room, Billy would have some time to himself. Though he might be called to the Queen Mother's private rooms at any point in the afternoon and evening – it rarely occurred to her that he might be tired or need some time off.

Occasionally, after these luncheons, Billy would spend a short while with the Queen Mother going over the details of the lunch. Sometimes she would ask Billy to put a record on and insist that he waltz around her private sitting room. Billy always claimed she could waltz him off his feet even into her eighties, and she

liked to make jokes about their dancing together. She would say
'We really are a sprightly pair of old girls, aren't we, William?' or
'Shall we dance out into the Mall? Wouldn't that surprise every-
one? One's relatives would not be amused.'

The truth is that the Queen Mother liked to blur the distinction between William her page and William her friend, which
is why if no lunch had been organised she would invite William
to lunch with her tête à tête. On another occasion after a particularly successful evening party, Billy accompanied the Queen
Mother to one of the sitting rooms where records were played
and in a remarkable moment of spontaneity the Queen Mother
insisted Billy sit next to her.

But if the Queen Mother went to lie down after lunch Billy
might help himself to bottles of unfinished (and frequently
unopened) wine and head off slightly unsteadily to his rooms
(and later to Gate Lodge), where he would sleep for an hour or
two. There was nothing irregular about his taking wine – it was
accepted that he would do so and the last person who might have
objected was the Queen Mother.

FROM AN HISTORICAL perspective, it was traditional
in the afternoon for all servants to have a few hours free
before the serious work connected with the family's wining and
dining began in the evening. It was just the same, in theory, for
Billy and the other servants at Clarence House.

Eric Gray, who worked with Billy for a short while in the early 1970s, recalls that Billy's weekday routine was fairly strict, but that things were often very different in the evening or if the Queen Mother was away and Billy had been left to 'look after the cat' as he used to put it.

> Each day after lunch Billy disappeared to his rooms unless the Queen Mother had asked him to do something in particular – it might just be a request to collect a trinket from somewhere or other – which did occasionally happen. But if the request had to do with the corgis or junior staff, Billy would often get Reg to do it – Reg never complained because he wasn't the complaining sort and, besides, Billy was his boss. The junior staff, especially the young men, liked Reg but sometimes disliked or at least feared Billy, who could come across as stern or bitchy if he didn't like you.
>
> When Reg had finished with the junior staff he might join Billy upstairs in his rooms and there was a joke in the house that staff should avoid going anywhere near Billy's part of the house when Reg was up there in case we heard any noisy lovemaking!

But Billy also liked to walk around St James's in the afternoon 'in his full regalia' as Reg used to say. He liked to be seen leaving the building as often as possible because the duty policeman would always nod respectfully and it made Billy feel as if he really was a VIP, which in a way he was. He liked going to Berry Bros, the royal wine shop, in St James's, where he was well known, and to Locks the hatters, a place he adored because of its history and its extraordinarily attentive staff. But wherever he went he was treated with the kind of reverence normally reserved for the aristocracy. Oddly, his desire to be noticed didn't make him a figure of fun. He was respected because it was widely known that the Queen Mother, though she might tell him off discreetly now and then, could not do without him. A common joke about Billy ran, 'We know which old queen is really in charge here, and it isn't the QM!'

Various servants of the time who saw Billy and the Queen Mother together when no one else was around noted that there was something of the devoted couple about them. 'They had any number of private jokes that no one else understood,' recalled one. Some people said it was more like Labrador and master but it was common knowledge that they enjoyed little intimate chats and Billy would whisper jokes and little asides in her ear. She was as intimate with Billy as she was with anyone.

This is why she famously lost her temper – a very rare thing – with one of the equerries. He had fallen out with Billy and tried to impose his will, not just on Billy but also on the Queen Mother. She responded by telling the equerry, 'Your job is negotiable; William's is not.'

Former servant Eric Gray remembered one of those moments when Billy and the Queen Mother seemed especially like a long-married couple.

> When I helped in the dining room, on several occasions I saw the Queen Mother and Billy having a very intimate kind of conversation.

She would smile and sometimes laugh at what he said but he had an incredible sense of just how far he could go. He rarely got it wrong. Although he would at times lean close to her, he was never over-familiar, which I don't think she would have liked at all, and he was very good with words – very witty in a dry clever way that was camp, but not irritatingly so. I once heard Billy speaking to the Queen Mother as one of her rather boring equerries approached along the corridor. Billy whispered audibly, 'O la di bloody da, here she comes'. I think it was a slip as Billy avoided more obviously camp stuff in front of the Queen Mother. He went slightly red but the Queen Mother hooted with laughter and I could see Billy was pleased – and perhaps surprised.

Billy's working day rarely ended before eleven at night, for the Queen Mother enjoyed her social life enormously through the 1970s and 1980s before age began to take its toll. Fuelled by her favourite Tanqueray gin she could keep going for hours on end and was often heard to say there was no point going to bed early as she had nothing to get up for in the morning. Typically, it never occurred to her that other people, especially the servants, were not so lucky.

When the day finally ended at Clarence House, Billy, dressed as ever in his white tie and tails, would politely open the door to the Queen Mother's private quarters and, having bowed her in, he would retire to bed. That at least is what appeared to be happening. The Queen Mother knew that Billy might well go up to his room after leaving her; she also knew that on many nights he had no intention of staying in his room. Instead he changed his clothes, trotted quietly down the back stairs and out past the policeman into the night.

Chapter Twelve

On the prowl

BILLY'S CHARACTER WAS created to a large extent by his highly developed sex drive. He had a good solid relationship with his partner Reg but after their initial passion cooled and a lifelong friendship developed, Billy still felt the irresistible pull of night-time adventuring.

As one contemporary, whom Billy seduced a few hours after he started work at Clarence House, said:

Billy was two completely different people. He was calm and almost rigidly decorous during the day, for the most part. Charming and discreet with lovely manners, he could make anyone feel good about themselves, but at night he had only one aim and that was to have sex with as many boys as possible. I don't think it is fair to say, as some have said, that he was predatory, in the sense that he would force people to do things they didn't want to do, but let's put it like this – he could be very persuasive! This was especially true when it came to fellow servants, because he knew he had a certain amount of power over them, although I don't think he ever used that power, at least he didn't early on when he was still young and good looking. He mostly didn't have to.

The truth is that Billy's only real interest outside his work was sex. Sex, as I've said, with as many boys as possible. This might sound shocking, but in those pre-AIDS days in the 1960s and 1970s it was common for highly sexed young gay men to see sex as an end in itself. They rejected the bourgeois idea that you should only have sex with someone with whom you had formed a relationship. And to be fair, the same ideas permeated heterosexual people at that time – sex was a great liberator for all until AIDS terrified everyone into domesticity.

Even Billy's staunchest supporters admit that his sexual appetites were extraordinary, and they seemed hardly to diminish even as he entered his fifties and sixties.

When Billy left Clarence House late in the evening, instead of his formal butler's suit – tail coat, white tie and plenty of medals – he would don a casual jacket and trousers. But there was nothing subtle about this transformation. He loved contrasting colours and might well wear a green tweed coat with purple trousers and an orange shirt. For those used to seeing him in his formal attire, the change was striking. He was virtually unrecognisable, as a fellow servant recalled. 'I spotted him on the stairs once and thought "Who the bloody hell is that?" I did a double take and then realised it was William in what looked very much like fancy dress!'

Once out into the Mall, Billy had two favourite routes. One of them was to walk up St James's Street and along Piccadilly to Hyde Park Corner, which, in the 1950s and early 1960s, was a favourite haunt of gay men looking for other men.

Like the Labour Peer Lord Bradwell (better known as Tom Driberg, 1905–1976), with whom he may well have had a brief affair, Billy was far keener on oral rather than any other kind of sex – according to one of his chance encounters, Billy seemed to think that swallowing large quantities of semen was the secret of eternal youth.

Don Jones, who knew Billy well around this time, said:

> Billy was one of a number of queens who didn't really like having sex done to him if you see what I mean – he liked doing it to others. Partly because of the idea that sperm – especially from young men – would keep him young but also because he always wanted to be in charge.
>
> I think his desire for control was linked to the influence of his strong-willed mother. She was the tough one. He liked strong women, which is why he stayed with the Queen Mother for so long, but he didn't like strong men who might compete with him. I think his father

was much less of an influence. Billy definitely took after his mother. Today we would say he was in touch with his maternal side but it was a pretty fierce and sometimes controlling maternal side.

But when it came to cruising for sex, he was no different really from thousands of other young gay men in London at that time. It's easy to be unkind about him now that he's dead [but] I don't think he was particularly predatory or irresponsible. He was just part of a scene that was very promiscuous. It was also furtive and anonymous and harked back to the days before homosexuality was legalised. You have to remember that Billy was in his thirties before homosexuality ceased to be a crime. In the old days, cottaging was one of the few ways gay men could get sex with the minimum risk of being caught. But even when it was no longer necessary, a lot of older men and some young ones still found it more exciting than meeting men in a bar or in some other, more conventional way. It was exciting because it was slightly dangerous. When homosexuality between consenting adults was legalised in the mid-1960s I think Billy, like a lot of gay men, was a little disappointed. Without the danger some of the fun had gone.

But Billy was also fascinated by other kinds of sex. He was intrigued by reports that Oscar Wilde had enjoyed 'crus sexus' – he was delighted to discover that this involved simply rubbing one's thigh against another man's genitals. 'Very poetic, I'm sure,' he used to say.

If Billy decided not to go to Hyde Park his favoured route was usually along the Mall to Green Park, Victoria and on to Kennington, where he was to spend his last years.

He also liked Soho, which was, in its heyday in the 1960s and 1970s, a magnet for people such as the painter Francis Bacon and writer Daniel Farson, who held court in Wheelers and the Colony Room. But Billy was always discreet so far as it was possible to be discreet when you were on the prowl, and he always made sure he was back at Clarence House in time to get just enough sleep to be ready for his duties next morning. Nonetheless, he drove himself hard. For years he had too little sleep and drank heavily yet never missed a day's work.

'He was immensely strong,' recalled a fellow servant. 'We used to say he had the constitution of an ox, although I think the years of debauchery did begin to tell even before the tremendous shock of losing his job and his home after the Queen Mother's death. I can remember his hand sometimes shook and he had a permanently red face.'

Occasionally Billy's natural caution would be abandoned and his carefully concealed love of risk and danger bubbled to the surface. His friends said he was both drawn to risk and repelled by it. In many ways he loved danger – the risk of being found out – because it had been so much a part of his earliest amorous adventures in London in the 1950s, but he knew that taking risks too often could destroy his career and put an end to his nights on the town. The riskier side of sex never quite outweighed his love for his career.

If the Queen Mother was away, which happened several times a year, all her staff – at least those who remained at Clarence House – heaved a sigh of relief. 'You could feel the atmosphere change in a moment,' recalled one. 'We went from a kind of heightened tension to a relaxed but almost deflated atmosphere where we chatted to each other more and had more free time, but missed the excitement of the Queen Mother being around.'

Noel Kelly, who knew Billy well at this time, remembered how Billy operated:

> Well, Billy would go out in the evening 'to see friends' as he used to say but we all knew he was probably looking for a pick-up. It is true that he did have a remarkable number of friends, especially in the world of theatre and ballet, but he didn't see them that often and I don't think they knew him at all intimately – no one really knew Billy intimately in the sense of understanding what really made him tick.

Billy must have known that his indiscretions were a continual source of delight to the below-stairs gossipers. After all, he liked gossip as much as anyone. But he relied on his position to protect him from any direct challenge.

'I'm sure Billy didn't really think the policeman at the gate believed him when he claimed that a very dodgy-looking character shiftily hanging back behind him was an old friend he was simply bringing in for tea,' remembered Noel Kelly. The policemen knew that so long as Billy had the confidence of the Queen Mother, they couldn't challenge anyone he chose to take on a tour of the house.

> Once or twice Billy told the policemen that the boy he was with was a cousin or even a nephew and the policemen would always nod

them through. Part of the appeal of doing this was not just the danger of taking a boy into Clarence House. It was also an exercise of power. Billy knew that the sort of boys he picked up would be astonished and impressed that they were about to get a tour of one of the world's most famous houses.

One of Billy's boyfriends explained that, in the gay bars of Soho, Billy was famous for his standard chat-up line.

He'd eye someone up and offer to buy him a drink. Then when they got talking he would calmly ask what the boy did. Most of the young men around Soho at that time were aspiring or out-of-work actors or they were hoping to break into the fashion or advertising industries. A few claimed they were models or artists. Everyone knew that we all lied about what we did but no one cared. If you wanted to be an actor or a model – if that's what you aspired to – then it was fine to say you actually *were* an actor or a model.

Then along comes Billy and calmly slips into the conversation that he is a senior member of staff at Clarence House. If that didn't impress – and some young men would never have understood the significance of the words Clarence House – Billy would explain that he worked in a personal capacity for the Queen Mother. Of course the boys on first acquaintance assumed this too was just fantasy – just another tale told in the bars. We all just wanted to impress each other. So when Billy was met with a sceptical smile, he would say, 'Why don't you come back to the house for tea and you can see?'

Very few could resist that kind of an invitation. So they would trot off on the twenty-minute walk back to the palace. The first time I went back with Billy I remember thinking as we got closer to Clarence House, 'He really must work there or he would have made a joke by now about inventing the whole thing'. Many people would spin you a line and then make a joke about fiction being much more interesting than fact or they would say, 'I would say anything to get *you* into bed!'

But Billy was different. He marched into the courtyard with me in tow, shaking in my boots. I daren't look at the policeman on the gate but Billy had the air of a recently crowned king. I hardly noticed any-thing as we walked through several corridors and up a staircase and then we were in what I thought was a very grand room. There was also an old wooden lift that Billy mostly used, but that first time we took the stairs for some reason.

I found myself in Billy's sitting room, but compared to my bed-sit in Camberwell this was very smart. Having talked about working in the palace when we met, he now refused to answer any searching questions about what exactly he did. I asked a few things about the Queen Mother but he gave nothing away beyond that he worked for her. I thought this was odd after he'd actually brought me into the old girl's house! I was quite drunk by this time but he carefully poured two glasses of a delicious red wine and asked about me. I thought he was very polite but it was probably just to stop me asking any more questions about him.

Next minute he made a rather crude lunge at me, which I didn't mind – it was almost comic and besides I was used to that kind of thing. He wasn't a great lover, I have to say – my memory is that it was all over in about five minutes.

Billy didn't quite kick me out afterwards but he looked a little bored and I knew better than to ask if I could stay. He saw me to the gate and off I went!

Other men picked up by Billy were not so well behaved and on several occasions after he saw his visitor to the door he would discover that one or two of his possessions were missing. He accepted this with good grace but was furious on another occasion when one of his visitors wandered off on his own for an unscheduled tour of the house.

Rita Edwards, who was a maid at Clarence House, recalled how she was horrified late one night to bump into a stranger in the house who was clearly completely lost.

I stopped dead when I saw this well-dressed young man looking at one of the paintings. I'd never seen him before and I was so surprised that I simply froze. We always knew who to expect to see even during the day so for there to be a stranger alone in the house at night was a serious security breach. Before I could decide what to do, I saw Billy suddenly at the far end of the corridor. His hair was all over the place and he was trying to put his jacket on as he stumbled along the corridor – I'd never seen him so flustered. He quickly reached the young man and was clearly furious, though he tried to control his features. The two of them wandered back the way Billy had come. Next time we met he made absolutely no reference to this embarrassing night-time escapade. But that was so typical of him. He would simply float above any difficulty or embarrassment. He may have known that the young man's presence would be talked about in the servants' hall but so long as no one ever spoke to him about it he didn't mind what other people said.

Chapter Thirteen

A dangerous character

T HOUGH FONDLY REMEMBERED as a genial character by many of those who knew him, Billy, as we have seen, had a darker side. Few of his female friends saw this side of him because he never felt threatened by women, especially those women like Reta Michael who perhaps reminded him of his mother.

Fellow servants, on the other hand, and especially if they were male, were sometimes perceived by Billy as a potential threat to his position and he found this unbearable because one of the greatest pleasures in his life – a pleasure he would rather die than give up – was the exercise of power, especially over his subordinates at Clarence House. This was fine so long as he liked those who worked under him. He was, as it were, a benevolent despot. He was also supportive and considerate to many of his fellow servants, but, inevitably, with a large turnover of staff and a tremendous mix of different characters, there were those with whom Billy simply could not get on. Some he really hated. And as even the grandees such as Aird and Anstruther found, Billy was a force to be reckoned with if he decided you were the enemy.

If the gin and wine were delayed or the flowers didn't look quite fresh each day, Billy was perhaps entitled to be cross with the more junior staff, but there is no doubt that he used his senior position occasionally to exploit junior members of staff if he felt attracted to them. He would never have tried anything sexual with young men from Eton and Oxford, but junior footmen and others were fair game. And, of course, the distinction between his private life and his professional life was dangerously blurred.

Most of his sex life was focussed on night-time Soho but one of Clarence House's great advantages was not just that it offered him a magnificent home where he was surrounded by luxury. It was also a place that, as we have seen, made available in varying degrees a string of innocent young men away from home, just starting work and sleeping on the premises.

Billy's unrestricted access to the Clarence House cellars provided a key tool in his seduction kit. 'As long as he didn't actually fall over in front of her she didn't mind a bit how drunk he was,' recalled one fellow servant.

This combination of opportunity – a selection of regularly changing young men sleeping under the same roof as Billy – alcohol and a powerful sexual urge was bound to lead to trouble.

FORMER ROYAL SERVANT Liam Cullen-Brooks remembered Billy's darker side.

Cullen-Brooks started work at Clarence House in 1992 aged nineteen. Like Billy, he remembered being fascinated by the royal family as a child. He'd watched various royal ceremonies on television and, as soon as he was old enough, jumped at the chance to move to a job at Clarence House. He started as a junior footman and was interviewed by Billy. Right from the start he felt that Billy was a man with two sides – it was a classic case, he recalled, of Dr Jekyll and Mr Hyde. Throughout that initial interview Billy maintained what Liam recalled as a 'cheesy grin' and the interview appears to have amounted to little more than an informal chat.

All went well initially for Liam but it was not long before he began to see a side of Billy that was carefully concealed from the Queen Mother and the senior staff.

According to Cullen-Brooks, Billy wasn't just fond of a drink. He was habitually drunk and when drunk he couldn't control himself. He was, according to Liam, vicious and vindictive and very much a sexual predator.

Other former male servants have confirmed the general picture of Billy as occasionally lecherous. One said:

> Billy offered young men jobs if he fancied them and no sooner had they started work than he turned his often unwanted sexual attentions on them. If they failed to respond he could make life very difficult indeed. To be fair he could be very charming if he liked you – even if you gave him the brush-off when he made it clear that he was sexually interested in you – but sometimes the devil got into him and he simply would not take no for an answer.

According to Cullen-Brooks, Billy was a man determined to be king in his own little empire and ruthless in his determination to crush anyone who questioned his authority or failed to comply with his wishes.

Like all the Clarence House servants, Liam worked tremendously long hours, from early morning until perhaps eleven or later in the evening. This was an Edwardian, perhaps even Victorian, world where workers' rights were notable by their absence. Staff were given to understand that if they didn't like the conditions there were always others ready to replace them.

But Cullen-Brooks discovered, as Billy had done all those years ago, that there was at least one major compensation – Liam's tiny salary was supplemented by free accommodation: a small room at the top of the house.

Generally speaking the Queen Mother lived at Clarence House during the week and then set off each weekend for Royal Lodge in Windsor Great Park. Here a largely new team of servants was always on hand to look after her. Billy and perhaps one or two others often, though by no means always, accompanied her when she went away. If they stayed at home then Liam, Billy and the other servants were left to their own devices.

For young isolated male servants staying in London, weekends could be very difficult to negotiate. Up to seven young junior butlers worked under Billy and Reg and on quiet weekends there was always a risk that Billy would pounce. Reg was never accused of being a 'pouncer' but even his best friends would probably agree that Billy, though charming, was not so gentle.

'If he wanted you, I mean sexually, he made it clear that you wouldn't be at all popular if you turned him down,' recalled one former junior butler.

By the mid-1970s Billy had long ago moved out of his bed-sitting room at the top of the house to Gate Lodge. It was rumoured that one reason for Billy's move was that the Queen Mother didn't want him bringing boys into the main house at all hours. With his little bungalow well away from the main building, Billy could get people in and out without anyone noticing. All the Queen Mother apparently ever said was, 'You mustn't be too naughty in your free time, William.'

David Smith, who left Clarence House after being pursued by Billy, recalled a man whose seduction technique was ruthlessly efficient.

It was shortly after Billy moved to his little lodge that I started work.

He was incredibly friendly at first and as I'd just left home and felt slightly lost I found his charm irresistible. He spoke very gently in what sounded to me like a very posh accent. He wasn't pompous like the senior advisers and he didn't talk down to me. I was such an innocent that I thought he must be like this with everyone. I sensed a slight change when he suggested one day that I go for tea at Gate Lodge in the afternoon. I thanked him but declined because I thought I should write a few letters home and go for a walk. In truth I didn't want to spend my free time talking about work, which is what I thought we'd inevitably end up doing, but when I said no Billy's manner changed very subtly. 'You really must come, you know,' he said, and I could tell he really meant that this was an order not an invitation.

The first thing David noticed when he arrived at Gate Lodge was the carefully designed and rather beautiful interior. The walls were covered with pictures and signed photographs of many of the royals and of theatre people. Billy loved ornaments and they were everywhere, along with numerous sofas and chairs. There was an impression of clutter, but then the rooms were tiny with very low ceilings, which added to a slight effect of claustrophobia. David and other visitors thought the rooms looked exactly like those of the ladies in waiting. It was surprisingly feminine.

Billy 'made a grab' for David at some stage, but 'it was just a sort of vague fumble and all over in a minute'.

I was slightly bewildered rather than offended, but he never invited me to tea again. I know some people have said he was a bully but he

didn't really bully me – it was more a subtle intimidation. I was also
a very passive sort of person in those days – very inexperienced – and
just gave in to him that afternoon at Gate Lodge.

The one thing all those who knew Billy would agree about is that
he was an enormously complicated character and that the com-
plexity was the result of his various different and largely separate
lives: his childhood in Coventry, his promiscuous gay side and his
serious would-be upper-class role in Clarence House. He was also
something of an artist – everyone said it about him. Gate Lodge
reflected his taste and everything he did for the Queen Mother
was done with a kind of artistic flourish.

REG WILCOX WAS in many ways the complete opposite of Billy. He was unambitious, serene and, apparently,
always happy. He could smooth over almost any difficulty and
when Billy had a tantrum it was always Reg who would calm
him down. It was also Reg, calm, kind and seemingly loved by
all, who handed the Queen Mother her tea on the morning of
her one hundredth birthday.

As the Queen Mother's Deputy Steward and Page of the Presence, Reg was, at least formally, Billy's subordinate, but in the
hothouse world of Clarence House below stairs such distinctions
mattered less than personal relationships. It was the intense personal and emotional relationship between Reg and Billy that really

mattered. They were soulmates and life partners to the extent that Reg was only occasionally perturbed by Billy's promiscuous nature.

Johnny Hewitt, who knew Billy well at this time, explains:

> Many people have claimed that Reg and Billy worked as a sort of team – a team of sexual predators. I don't think that was true at all. It was part of Reg's character to be intensely loyal both in terms of his job and his personal relationships. Billy was always intensely loyal to his employer, the Queen Mother, but he was not so loyal in his personal relationships.
>
> Reg was aware that Billy was promiscuous, but he didn't really mind. He accepted people for what they were to a remarkable degree. I think this is why Reg was famous among staff and royals for his wonderful good temper and refusal to judge. He was actually far more highly rated than Billy, except of course by the Queen Mother. If Billy was loyal it was perhaps to the 95 per cent mark. Reg was 100 per cent loyal. Even the rather serious and formal Aird and Anstruther found it almost impossible to say a harsh word about Reg, and the ladies in waiting and other staff loved him.

Others noted that Reg only really felt safe and entirely himself when surrounded by stronger characters such as Billy. If Billy was later to find it difficult to live outside in the real world, Reg would have found it impossible.

It is generally agreed that the occasional bullying and spitefulness of life below stairs in Clarence House was a product of rigid social stratification. Servants in the royal household were in many ways more concerned about their status than the people for whom they worked. Where the royals felt superior to those who were not from the same or a very similar set, the upper servants felt superior to the lower servants. It was all about hierarchy, whether you were a member of the family or one of the staff. And if the atmosphere was sometimes unkind it could also be intensely rewarding, as the hothouse conditions that destroyed some relationships sealed others for life.

Chapter Fourteen

Sudden enthusiasms

THOUGH THERE WERE many quiet week-ends with the Queen Mother away at her various country houses, Billy was less often left to his own devices than other servants simply because he was the Queen Mother's favourite. There was something about Billy's skill as an adviser, his tact and discretion as a friend that increasingly led to a situation where the Queen Mother just did not feel happy if he was not around. This bolstered Billy's sense of power; his sense that when it came to the other servants he could more or less do as he liked.

His close friend Basia Briggs believes that power was an important part of Billy's make-up: 'I think he loved power. He loved the fact that he was untouchable because of his importance to the Queen Mother and he very often exercised the power that position gave him.'

Another friend agrees: 'I think he had more influence in some ways over the Queen Mother than any member of the royal family, let alone the overly serious advisers, and of course for that they disliked him intensely. This is perhaps why when he died no immediate member of the royal family attended his funeral.'

A number of Billy's fellow servants have argued, unkindly perhaps, that Billy's greatest skill was actually sycophancy; others have said that the Queen Mother was far too shrewd to enjoy the company of someone who simply agreed with everything she said. In fact she notably disliked those who too obviously tried to curry favour and Billy was acutely aware of this.

The truth is that Billy was enormously skilful at mixing amusing conversation with risqué comments and solid dependability. It was Billy she turned to when discussing who and what to take to the Castle of Mey or on her trips overseas. The arrangements might have been made by Anstruther and Aird but she would never ask them to organise her store of gin for the journey or discuss which dogs to take or leave behind. Their contribution would have made the preparations dull; Billy's contribution was to make everything interesting and fun.

Before one trip to Scotland, Billy spent a morning discussing arrangements with the Queen Mother, who seemed to be unusually flustered about arrangements that varied little between each visit. Billy became slightly exasperated and the Queen Mother said, 'William, we don't want this to turn into a muddle, do we?'

William said, 'Yes, ma'am, or even a bugger's muddle.'

Barely able to suppress her giggles, the Queen Mother merely replied, 'Well, quite.'

This was typical of Billy and he was also capable of childish enthusiasms and sudden bursts of hilarity which the rather serious Aird and Anstruther simply could not comprehend. They perhaps felt, as Queen Victoria's advisers had felt more than a century earlier, that beyond a bit of Scottish country dancing, the Queen Mother's fun should consist of polite and very restrained conversation. With Billy she could forget all this; in her public life she had far too much polite small talk, so in private she wanted no polite small talk at all. She wanted someone who would make scathing and sometimes very funny remarks about the 'old bores' upstairs, someone who would say, as Billy once said about a new press secretary, 'I like him very much, but then I have absolutely no taste.'

Despite his reputation as a raconteur, which was largely deserved, Billy could also sometimes be a bore.

'It all depended on the company he found himself in,' recalled one friend.

> I remember going to a party in Highgate in the early 1990s where there were far fewer people than Billy and I had expected. There were I think six of us at the table, five very obviously gay men and one woman. It

was all fine at first but then the alcohol began to take effect and every single thing that was said by the men was a very crude double entendre. The first few were probably genuinely funny, but as time went on they became more obscene and less funny and the poor woman, who was an old friend of Billy's, looked bored out of her wits by the end. And I must say I had every sympathy with her. The problem was that occasionally Billy loved this kind of smutty rather juvenile humour.

On one occasion Billy found himself waiting behind the Queen Mother's writing table while she looked through her correspondence. One of the equerries knocked and came in to ask about a meeting later that day. When the equerry had left the room the Queen Mother asked Billy if he had had a chance yet to get to know him. Billy made a face as if he was sucking a lemon and the Queen Mother was delighted. But occasionally he misjudged things. He had been making teasing remarks about one of the elderly equerries being remarkable in that he was still able to sit up and hold a spoon. The Queen Mother told Billy his remarks were out of place.

It was a telling reminder of something the Queen Mother often said of herself: 'I'm not as nice as I look.' And a number of other stories reveal someone who could be delightful but also occasionally waspish and eccentric.

Noel Kelly recalled that Billy enjoyed telling amusing stories of how the Queen Mother had muddled something, behaved in an odd way or asked him to do the impossible. He was particularly fond, it seems, of a story involving the Queen Mother and the late Lord Callaghan.

The Queen Mother had rather liked Callaghan, recalled Billy, so he was a frequent guest at Clarence House. On one occasion, when she and Callaghan were alone, she happened to be eating (almost continuously) from an enormous box of chocolates. She offered him a chocolate and when he said yes, she pointed to a particular chocolate and made it clear that he could have that one and no other.

While he munched his way through his chocolate she popped one after another into her own mouth and then after some time offered him another chocolate. Just to see what would happen he again said yes and once again she pointed to a particular chocolate and told him he could only have that one. Callaghan later asked one of the pages why on earth he had been offered those particular chocolates and no others. Then came the solemn reply: 'Those are the ones with hard centres. Her Majesty only eats the chocolates with soft centres.'

BASIA BRIGGS REMEMBERED an occasion when the Queen Mother and her lady in waiting, Lady Fermoy, upset Billy during an argument in the garden. He stormed off and Lady Fermoy called after him ordering him to come back at once. He took no notice and when he finally returned ten minutes later Lady Fermoy told him he was the bravest man in the country. No one else would have defied the Queen Mother in this way.

'I think in some ways she was definitely rather in love with

Billy,' recalled Noel Kelly. 'We all thought it. It was partly the result of the fact that she knew he adored her and partly because he was the only person in the household who seemed to her to be in touch with the bawdy, funny, irreverent world outside the horribly closed-up, serious world of the royals. He also stood up to her now and then as no one else ever did and he reminded her of the fun and gaiety of the 1920s, which is where she really lived. She loved the music of that era and she wanted her life as much as possible to contain the things that she had at that time that enabled her to forget about the horrors of the Great War in which she lost her brother Fergus. In some ways Billy's manner, his humour and ability to talk well reminded her of the carefree balls and parties she had attended as a girl.'

And Billy responded to what he saw as a mix of the skittish girl, the matriarch and the emotionally needy in the Queen Mother – which is why when he was occasionally left at home in London when she went to Scotland or abroad he partly enjoyed it and partly hated it.

What he really loved was the world of show business; a world equally loved by the Queen Mother herself. And Billy made a point of keeping in touch with anyone he liked from this or any other world. Basia Briggs recalled being invited to lunch with the Queen Mother as a result of her involvement in the design of a new set of gates at Hyde Park Corner. The Queen Elizabeth Gate, designed by David Wynne, one of the Queen Mother's favourite artists, was installed to celebrate the Queen Mother's ninetieth birthday. Billy escorted Basia into the specially organised lunch and, as Basia recalls, 'we just seemed to hit it off'. At the end of lunch Billy escorted her out again but made a point of asking for her phone number and promising he would stay in touch, which is exactly what he did. 'He always did this with people he felt he liked,' she recalled.

Many of Billy's friends were actors from the Queen Mother's favourite TV shows, especially Patricia Routledge of *Keeping Up Appearances* fame.

⁂

A S T H E Y E A R S passed and long hours and alcohol took their toll, Billy began to slow down. He became less sexually voracious and his night-time adventures became less frequent. He retained an echo of his remarkable early good looks but his puffy red face became increasingly noticeable whenever he appeared in public with the Queen Mother.

He told one friend in the mid-1990s that he felt he was enjoying growing old with the Queen Mother although she was actually more than thirty years his senior. She and Billy had fewer tiffs as time went on and settled into a comfortable routine that was rarely disturbed by outside events. By the time she reached her ninetieth year, Billy's night-time activities were less of a worry too because his indiscretions with young men became to some extent a thing of the past. He became a more domestic creature – 'he was like an old family pet', as one contemporary recalled.

But age did not diminish his love of parties and indeed Gate

Lodge became legendary for its champagne-fuelled nights, as Basia Briggs remembered.

Billy absolutely adored parties and we enjoyed a seemingly endless stream of wonderful evenings at Gate Lodge. And he had so many friends from all walks of life. Gate Lodge was tiny but that didn't seem to matter a bit. It had a few rooms with very low ceilings but my memory is that it was always full of laughter and fun and people sitting on and in every available space.

Billy was a marvellous host. He was at his amusing best at these parties and they would go on until the early hours. I can remember as we would begin to leave we would be reminded that the Queen Mother's balcony was only a short distance away and as she slept with the window open in the summer we needed to be quiet. Everyone would immediately start to make shushing noises. But it was absurd because after so much champagne our attempts to keep each other quiet would themselves probably have woken the Queen Mother!

Billy also had remarkable energy even into his fifties and sixties. We might have been drinking and partying all afternoon and evening but if someone suggested we go on to something else – another party, I mean – Billy would always go however late it might happen to be.

A neighbour who knew him in his last years recalled a characteristic evening.

Well, Billy loved to get a group of people together and then be the centre of attention. I don't mean that in a bitchy way because he was so much fun that everyone forgave his desire to be the life and soul. It's very hard to describe him at his best because although he could be witty and tell good stories it was much more to do with his sense of fun. He was like a child at a party who completely lets himself go and the effect was to make everyone else let themselves go. His parties were always very good because of this. If the host rushes about in a completely uninhibited way it's wonderfully liberating.

Regulars at Billy's local pub remembered that as the night wore on Billy would become increasingly drunk and outrageous, but he was never violent or offensive.

He would get everyone to join in the conversation and he would start talking in a completely open and somehow rather innocent way to absolutely anyone. It wasn't a result of being lonely although he was certainly that. It was more the habit of a lifetime carried over into a rough old pub in south London. When you knew what his job had been you could see that he was doing for us what he used to do for the Queen Mother at her lunches. He would talk to everyone to get them talking and enjoying themselves. He was a marvellous character. He was obviously gay, had a terrible dress sense – bright shirts and trousers that always clashed with each other – but because he was so friendly and open even the tough characters who were definitely gay haters – even they took to him.

Another friend who knew Billy for the last few years of his life recalled a quieter, more reflective character.

I was in my local pub one night when this guy in a bright yellow scarf and luminous green corduroy trousers sat down next to me. At first I was a bit wary. I thought, oh no, here comes the resident drunk who bores everyone to death, but within a few minutes I found myself opening up to him. He was a very likeable character. A natural talker and listener. Although I'm hopeless at talking to people I don't know well I found it very difficult *not* to talk to him.

Billy and his new friend became rather drunk and Billy invited him back to his flat where they carried on drinking.

It was when we got back to his flat – along with three other blokes from the pub – that I realised who he was. One of the other guys in our little party said, 'That's William Tallon, you know.' I told him the name didn't ring a bell at all. The other guy said, 'Worked for the Queen Mother for fifty years.' Anyway we had a great party. He invited me back regularly after that and I felt a great void in my life after he died, even though I never felt I knew him well. The point is you never felt you had to work hard to keep the conversation going. Billy just swept you along.

Other friends remember Billy's characteristic drawl.

'He still had a bit of his Coventry accent,' recalled one, 'but it was overlaid with a sort of nonchalant aristocratic twang.'

He would say about an acquaintance, 'Don't listen to a word he says. I know exactly what sort of creature he is. And do you know why? Well,

I will tell you. He was nothing before he met me. Absolutely nothing. But after a year or two with me he had polish. He was, you might say, semi divine,' and the word 'divine' would be long and drawn out; it was as if the word had about twenty-six letters in it! While he said it he would roll his eyes and pretend to flick back the hair on either side of his head. If he really wanted to emphasise the point he would finish a sentence, throw back his head, turn and stalk off. But he would be back in a second and ask, 'What did you think of that little performance?'

Another of his wonderfully entertaining little ploys was to shout across the room for silence and then he would announce that he was going to show us how to dance a few steps of flamenco, or an old-fashioned waltz. He would then cavort across the room to the huge delight of his audience. He was at these times completely uninhibited.

Another friend recalled how Billy's manner would change if some-one good-looking came along and he went into what his friends called 'chat-up mode'.

We were waiting in his flat for the plumber to arrive and when he did he was discovered to be rather good-looking so immediately Billy was on the alert. He became very attentive and interested in the young man. He asked him where he was from. The young man said, 'From Hornchurch.' Billy immediately responded by saying 'Oh, Horn-church,' with the sort of emphasis that made you think he had known Hornchurch all his life. The young man replied eagerly, 'Do you know it?' and Billy said, 'Good heavens. Of course not.' But he smiled and gave the young man a glass of champagne anyway.

Many of Billy's friends also noted his tendency to exaggerate wildly for effect. At one party given at Gate Lodge he told a guest that London was a bore now that he'd 'had everyone'. He then added, 'Well, anyone worth having, that is.'

He was also subject to sudden enthusiasms. If a party was going well he would sometimes ring a friend and persuade whoever it was to invite everyone at Gate Lodge – perhaps as many as twenty people – over to the friend's house. Once the person on the other end of the line had agreed, Billy would immediately call for half a dozen taxis and set off for Chiswick or Hampstead or wherever. Billy would lead the way out of Gate Lodge into the Mall with his arm held aloft; very much, as one friend put it, 'like a Japanese tourist group leader'.

On one occasion he told his friends they were all going to a party in Barnes. He organised the taxis and in great excitement the party set off. It was only as they crossed Hammersmith Bridge that Billy realised he should have told the taxi drivers to go to Balham. But, delighted at his mistake, he made a huge joke of it and simply told the taxi driver to turn round and head in another direction.

Billy often pulled the same trick in retirement in Kennington. He would invite half a dozen people home to his flat from the local pub and then ring a friend – sometimes a rather grand theatrical friend – and try to get an invitation for his new friends to visit then and there. It was usually the case that the people sitting round expectantly really were new friends – Billy had never set eyes on them before that evening. He would claim on the phone that they were all old friends. 'He was quite wild about that kind of thing,' recalled a regular at his local pub, the Dog House. 'He would get caught up in the moment – a moment made more reckless by a great deal of alcohol!'

As he grew older he became wilder in his habits and conversation but also less concerned about his appearance. He would dress up carefully in his last years at Clarence House but if he spilled food or more usually wine down his front he would make only perfunctory efforts to get rid of the stains.

'His beautiful suit was often covered in what looked like food and wine stains,' recalled a fellow servant. 'I once went into his office and found him using a black biro to try to blot out a white stain on his trousers. He wasn't in the least embarrassed that I'd seen him.'

Another servant explained that Billy had a rather unorthodox technique for keeping his hair looking youthful.

'He hated going grey when it first started to happen but was very lazy about getting it professionally dyed so he would brush dark brown boot polish through it just to hide the grey streaks. It actually worked very well!'

And Billy had other eccentric habits. He went through a period, for example, when he was convinced someone was tampering with the royal collection of Fabergé eggs. He became obsessive about checking them, a habit that was soon extended to the royal pictures, the various display cabinets and their contents, even the furniture.

'He admitted he had a bit of a problem,' recalled a fellow servant.

He thought it was because he was going through an anxious period, which might well have been true. But, on the other hand he was always at the centre of gossip, backbiting and intrigue so you'd have thought that he'd have been used to it. I mentioned to another servant that I thought Billy was a bit over-stressed and it was showing itself in his obsession with checking all these things, but she just said, 'It's nothing to do with that. He's just bloody mad!'

Billy was always the centre of a swirling mass of stories, many of which bore very little relation to reality. Several of his friends testify to his enjoyment of the stories that were told about him and he would sometimes say, in response to a question about a particular story, 'Well, I don't remember that at all but I'm sure it must be true. It's exactly what I would have done under the circumstances. It's completely in character.'

If the story added to Billy's sense of his importance in the royal household he would glow and he would rarely contradict something that added to the Backstairs Billy legend.

BOTH THE QUEEN Mother and her most devoted servant became locked into a life of comfortable and comforting routine, but it was a routine that would ultimately have disastrous consequences for Billy. Many people find that retirement is difficult because they have lost the structure that routine provides. But this problem was particularly acute for Billy because his work routine filled his days, his evenings and many of his weekends.

Billy gave her flowers on her birthday but it was a token gesture as she received gifts each year from all over the world. But it was these little rituals – at lunch and breakfast on birthdays and other special occasions – that bound them together. No one knows what he whispered to her but he made a point of whispering even when it was not strictly necessary – it was a way of indicating to others that he had special privileges. She had occasionally complained that Billy did this too often, but increasingly as she grew older she seemed to enjoy the intimacy it implied. Billy's adoration was not lost on her.

Chapter Fifteen

Change and decay

FORMER SERVANTS, LADIES in waiting, equerries and other officials all seem to agree that the death of Reg Wilcox in 2000 was in some ways far more of a blow to Billy than the death of the Queen Mother. Though his night-time forays to Soho led to numerous casual liaisons, Billy's relationship with Reg was based on something more enduring. One former servant said they were like an old-fashioned royal couple themselves.

When others were around they were curiously formal with each other and both thought it was silly and rather suburban to worry about sexual fidelity. Reg knew Billy would never leave him despite the endless affairs. How could he? A casual pick-up would never understand the life of a royal servant and would never want a permanent relationship with a man who was tied not just to the Queen Mother but also to the very edifice of bricks and mortar in which she lived.

Reg was always happy to be Billy's deputy since their work differed very little in essentials from day to day and Billy was always careful not to pull rank on his partner. Noel Kelly remembered: 'They were remarkably skilful at working together because although everyone knew they were a couple they behaved towards each other in the corridors of Clarence House with a kind of seriousness that warned you not to treat either of them lightly. Billy was fiercely protective of Reg and Reg was careful to defer to Billy but they worked together in a highly efficient way with Reg called upon only occasionally to smooth Billy's feathers.'

Noel Kelly recalled coming across the two men by chance in Clarence House. Billy was clearly very upset by something and Reg had his hand on Billy's forearm and was speaking calmly but very intently to him. They were so intent on each other that they didn't notice they had been spotted and in the time before they registered Kelly's presence he saw Billy's face go from almost black with rage to calm and almost sunny. It was an impressive performance. 'I've no idea what he said but whatever it was, it was precisely targeted and absolutely did the trick.'

The two men travelled regularly with the Queen Mother well into her eighties. Many of these trips were private affairs, especially to the Queen Mother's friends in France. Reg tended to organise while Billy was, as his friends often put it, front of house.

A well-known story recounts how the Queen Mother went to stay with a very grand friend in the south of France. Soon after she arrived she was shown to her room by her host. When the host opened the wardrobe, he was astonished to see that all the Queen Mother's things had already been carefully hung and laid out by Reg. On reaching the house he had immediately discovered who was responsible for the various practical arrangements and while the Queen Mother was still enjoying tea in the drawing room Reg had got to work. The Queen Mother apparently said to her astonished host, 'You see, I am here already.'

Holidays became much more difficult for the Queen Mother as she entered her nineties and in a curious parallel Reg and Billy stopped enjoying their occasional breaks together at around the same time. These had always been rather half-hearted affairs because the two men always felt slightly at a loss outside their working environment. It is easy to imagine that working six and a half, sometimes seven days a week and often long into the evening did not leave much time to develop outside interests beyond socialising and party going.

Additionally, as time went by Reg and Billy's lives became increasingly centred on Billy's little palace in the Mall and to a lesser extent on Reg's flat in Kennington where, occasionally at weekends, the couple did escape from Clarence House to tend their roses and sit out in the sun. The flat was actually Reg's but it was to provide a refuge – if sometimes an unhappy one – for Billy when his world finally collapsed.

❧ ❧

WITH RED-COATED SOLDIERS always guarding the gates next to Billy's Gate Lodge, it was one of his great pleasures to slip out when there were plenty of tourists about. He loved the fact that tourists immediately assumed he was a person of importance in the royal household, which of course he was. The cameras would start snapping in a frenzy when he appeared at his door and paused – deliberately and rather theatrically – before heading through the gate into the grounds of Clarence House or out and along the Mall. Billy would adopt an air of royal mystery before disappearing into the crowd.

Basia Briggs tells a marvellous story about leaving a garden party at Buckingham Palace and then walking along the Mall to Clarence House to see Billy and show him her hat. Soon afterwards she left Clarence House and, accompanied by Billy, waited to cross the Mall, which happened at that time to be very busy.

> Replete in his white tie and tails William got fed up waiting so he simply walked into the middle of the road with the traffic thundering all around him and held up his hand. The traffic came almost instantly to a standstill and I was able to cross. That was the sort of presence he had. He was convinced they would stop and so they did!

Such extravagant gestures did not always work, however. Billy loved to tell the story of how, crossing the Mall one day on his own, he once again held up his hand to stop the traffic. A Royal Parks lorry happened to have stopped by the kerb and the driver shouted through the window, 'Off to the fuckin' ball, are we, Cinderella?' Billy was about to reply when he noticed that a policeman had also heard the driver. Billy spoke to the policeman who cautioned the driver for using offensive language. Billy was delighted.

IKE BILLY, REG developed an interest in art (when he died it was discovered that he owned a number of valuable pictures) but he was far less voluble about it and in many ways he was rather a mystery. 'What on earth has he got to be so cheerful about?' asked one visitor to Clarence House when they heard Reg whistling and then singing one morning. But being cheerful was definitely Reg's trademark.

It is said that a rather grand equerry once reprimanded Reg in a high-handed way for singing and told him to keep quiet. A day or two later the equerry was astonished to receive a short letter from the Queen Mother telling him that Reg was permitted to sing and whistle whenever he chose and that the equerry should, though she did not say it in so many words, mind his own business. Moreover, Reg, despite his good nature, was not in any way a weak man or easily cowed. When the need arose he stood up for what he thought was right.

After a party at Balmoral, a group of drunken, rowdy guests who were all equerries or advisers began running along the corridors squirting soda siphons at each other. The Queen Mother was disturbed by the ruckus and commented that it was rather like being in the Blitz again. But Reg was indignant that her sleep had been disturbed and he informed the senior equerry that his behaviour would be reported to the Queen Mother's lady in waiting. The equerry was so surprised to be reprimanded in this way that he became red-faced and instantly stammered out his apologies, which, typically, Reg accepted with a good grace. Too kind to take it any further, Reg allowed the incident to be quietly forgotten.

ACCORDING TO BILLY, as the Queen Mother approached her centenary her mind began to fail. She may have looked the same to the public on her occasional appearances but in private she increasingly forgot things and became horribly muddled; she was also more prone to irritation, even where Billy was concerned.

It was the beginning of a decline that would lead eventually to Billy being kept completely apart from her during the last few months of her life. When she could no longer insist that Billy should continue to be her close companion – it is said she barely knew who or where she was during the last months of her life – the senior advisers made sure all the doors were locked against her former favourite.

As she entered her final decade her old habit of steeliness also became intensified. 'She had a tendency to look extremely firm – or steely – rather than to say anything. I don't think she liked directly reprimanding anyone,' recalled one of Billy's friends, 'but she sometimes took offence if Billy offered her his arm on public occasions. This had little to do with her feeling he was only a servant and therefore it was rather a presumptuous thing to do. It had far more to do with her wanting to seem fit enough to stand without aid even in extreme old age. She hated to seem weak when the cameras were rolling and the public were cheering.'

When the Queen Mother came out of Clarence House each year to greet the crowds on her birthday, Billy would often make every effort to get as close to her as possible. He would try to offer support only when she looked as if she was about to topple over. Inevitably he would occasionally misjudge things. Later he would get a stern look and she would say, 'William, I am not entirely incapable.'

William took this sort of mild rebuke in his stride, but he had a reputation for getting his revenge in subtle but highly effective ways with anyone else who crossed him.

If there happened to be a dispute with an equerry about some aspect of protocol, Billy would begin by discussing the issue in an oblique way with the Queen Mother. Once she had come round to Billy's view he would set off to see the relevant adviser, and explain that the Queen Mother wanted things in a certain way. It had nothing to do with Billy, of course; he was simply the messenger. And that would usually be the end of the argument.

But the Queen Mother would not live forever and Billy seems to have failed completely to realise that his high-handed behaviour would come back to haunt him. In the Queen Mother's last years he would have been wise to make fewer enemies and more friends. As it was, he did neither and his enemies were certainly plotting against him for at least a decade before she died. 'I think some of them even stayed on longer than they had originally planned just to see Billy get his comeuppance,' recalled one friend.

Billy's technique of using the Queen Mother's supposed views on a particular matter to get his way was also adopted by Reg and whenever a disagreement arose the staff knew it would not be long before Billy or Reg would be heard saying, 'Her Majesty prefers it that way.'

One servant recalled that 'half the time they were making it up and Her Majesty never got to hear about proposed changes to procedures. Reg and Billy would simply give the impression that the Queen Mother had been consulted on the proposals and had vetoed them.'

In 1998 Reg became seriously ill with leukaemia. The prognosis for childhood leukaemia is now very good but for those afflicted by the disease in middle age – Reg was just sixty-four – the prospects were, and still are, poor. Rumours circulated at the time that he was suffering from HIV or even full-blown AIDS and the situation was made worse when, already weakened by the disease that was eventually to kill him, Reg contracted a virus. But he was a tough character and seemed to have made a full recovery from both his leukaemia and his viral infection as the Queen Mother's one hundredth birthday approached. In fact he had been seriously weakened by his illnesses and only strength of will kept him going. He was determined, as Billy himself admitted tearfully in later years, to live until the Queen Mother reached her centenary.

One junior footman who knew him well during his last years said:

Everyone talks about Billy as the epitome of the faithful servant but Reg was the real thing. Billy took risks, drank too much and couldn't always control himself, where Reg seemed never to put a foot wrong. I sometimes used to think that Billy would have liked to be a star in his own right. I mean famous in some way independently of his association with the Queen Mother and occasionally you sensed that he regretted that the only way he could enjoy fame was through his association with the royals. You never got that impression with Reg. He didn't want the limelight – not even a small share of it – in the way that Billy did. But it was subtle differences like that that kept them happy together so long. If they'd both had big egos – and Billy's ego was huge! – they would never have got on so well.

But there are dissenting voices and at least one former servant, Liam Cullen-Brooks, paints a very different picture of both Reg and Billy. Liam felt that Billy was vindictive and would deliberately find fault if he happened to dislike someone. For example, he would double-check the cutlery and find fault with how well it had been cleaned even if it was spotless.

Liam particularly remembered an elderly under-butler whose

life was made an absolute misery. He was picked on continually by Billy and even by Reg. Liam claims it was like school playground bullying. Another servant who suffered badly from acne was teased mercilessly by Billy.

According to Liam, Billy would not just find fault; he would also make life difficult just for the sake of it. One servant was charged with clearing up the leaves that fell each night from a fig tree growing in a large pot by a set of doors. Billy would wait until the leaves had been cleared up, go back to the tree, shake it until more leaves had fallen and then berate the servant for not doing his job properly.

Liam also remembered the sense of shock when a diabetic servant collapsed on the terrace at Clarence House and Billy forbade anyone to touch him or help in anyway. He was simply left lying on the ground until an ambulance arrived. Billy is said to have simply stepped over the prostrate figure as he went about his work.

Various servants complained about Billy to Sir Alastair Aird, but to no avail. Billy was clearly seen as such a difficult character that little could be done to curb his excesses. There seems to have been an especially bad relationship between Billy and Reg and Betty Leek, who was for many years the Queen Mother's dresser and one of the few people who genuinely had more access to her than either of her pages. Billy would make snide remarks in a stage whisper as she passed and, goaded beyond endurance, she would eventually snap back. Billy would then make a formal complaint against her.

The extent to which the Queen Mother understood that Billy

had a dark side is difficult to determine, but she was no fool. One of her ladies in waiting is reported as having said that she knew that servants would always squabble and fall out: 'It's what servants had always done.'

Billy certainly made mistakes and he could be spiteful to those he did not like, but he also promoted those he liked and sometimes his desire to help his friends ended badly. Prince Charles's former valet Michael Fawcett, later the Prince's personal consultant, is a case in point. Billy was very keen that Fawcett should get the job of personal consultant because he liked him. Billy lobbied hard on his behalf and Fawcett got the job, but he was later forced to resign after a series of public embarrassments.

Billy and Reg did not have it all their own way, according to Liam. He recalls how now and then he got the better of Billy, Reg and their circle. He was once reprimanded by Michael Fawcett for laughing while breakfast was being prepared. Fawcett explained that Prince Charles had overhead and was annoyed. When Cullen-Brooks served lunch that day he made a point of apologising to Prince Charles for having laughed too loudly that morning. Charles was completely mystified and said that he hadn't been bothered in the least – that in fact he loved the sound of laughter.

Cullen-Brooks and other former members of the Clarence House staff also recall that on free weekends Reg and Billy would help themselves to wine and food from the Clarence House stores. Apparently the two men would tour the larders and cellars carrying a large bag which they would fill with wine and cheese and other delicacies before setting off for Reg's flat for the weekend.

The other servants referred to this as Billy and Reg's supermarket sweep, and it was something they apparently did regularly at Sandringham and Balmoral as well as at Clarence House.

Billy's usual habit at Balmoral was to pack a box of wine each week and post it to Reg in London. It was all part of Billy and Reg feeling they had special privileges because they had worked in the royal household for so long, and this was certainly reflected in Billy's increasingly erratic behaviour. He had always drunk heavily, but by the late 1990s he occasionally collapsed and had to be put to bed by Reg or one of the other servants.

These drunken episodes were very difficult to keep from the Queen Mother. The other servants would tell her that Billy was indisposed or ill and had gone to bed, but she clearly knew what was really going on and enjoyed teasing Billy about it.

After he re-appeared one morning looking decidedly the worse for wear she said: 'William, I hear you have not been feeling well. I had thought of sending up something to make you feel better. Perhaps some warm whisky and water. But then I thought no, perhaps not. Was I right not to?'

The temptations of royal service were huge. Salaries were tiny and it was the perks that made the job tolerable. And the perks were easy picking for Reg and Billy because they ordered food and wine as they pleased and never had to account for anything to anyone. Billy especially could take what he liked because the Queen Mother allowed him to order and dispose of whatever he liked.

'It was a good example of power corrupting,' recalled a former junior steward.

Reg and Billy would not have let anyone under them get away with what they got away with. They ran the household and took whatever they liked whenever they liked. Billy was the driving force and anyone they didn't get on with was definitely frozen out. If, on the other hand, you made an effort to get on with them and they liked you, then you would find you were part of the magic circle. They'd even give you the odd bottle of wine and some wonderfully expensive chocolates – and there were a lot of chocolates as the Queen Mother seemed to eat a dozen boxes a week.

In reality the arguments and disputes, the backbiting and resentments of servant life at Clarence House were probably typical of any environment where a disparate group is forced to live and work together.

As Noel Kelly put it:

It was a hothouse of intrigue, but what else could it be with all those strange and sometimes forceful personalities effectively locked up together? I think in some ways it was a bit like a prison or a public school with intense friendships and hatreds, petty disputes over privileges and an over-arching sense of claustrophobia. Very few people could survive it for long, which is why staff turnover was so high, but one or two, like Billy and Reg, actually thrived in that over-heated atmosphere.

WHEN REG WILCOX died in 2000, he left Billy just under £200,000 – much of it in the form of paintings – in his will. Like Billy, Reg had carefully collected gifts and pictures over the years, including a number of pictures by Billy's friend the artist Roy Petley. But Reg had also been popular with the Queen Mother and other royals and many people were surprised at how many valuable antiques he had accumulated. Some of these were left to Michael Fawcett, who had been a great friend.

For a while after Reg's death Billy drank even more than usual and seemed to lose some of his zest for life. 'The fire went out of him for a while,' recalled one friend. 'But the life force in him was so strong that he got over his bereavement remarkably well in the end. He even eased up a little, I think, on his drinking.'

He also threw himself into his relationship with the Queen Mother with even greater enthusiasm. Sometimes, staff would watch open mouthed as Billy, after one drink too many, would pick up one of the royal corgis in his arms and dance around with it, just as if it were his partner.

Billy also loved to tell the story of how the Queen Mother once caught a page sitting on a sofa next to Princess Margaret.

'What on earth is going on?' asked the Queen Mother. Margaret apparently replied, 'There is an unsightly hole in the sofa and I thought this was the best way to cover it up.'

Billy was scornful of stories run by the press detailing an incident in which he was said to have got into terrible trouble after Princess Margaret's final public appearance in August 2001. The newspapers saw that she was very ill and decided that Billy had made the decision to wheel her out in front of the public in a frightful condition.

'The idea that I would be the one to make such a decision is ridiculous,' said Billy. 'If Princess Margaret had asked to be there I could hardly have told her it was an inappropriate thing to do. She made these decisions, as did all the members of the family. I would not have dreamed of telling them what to do.'

Nonetheless, stung by newspaper reports that argued he had behaved very badly, Billy had written to the Queen, who responded with a hand-written letter telling him not to worry in the least.

And in the main, Billy did not worry about the decisions he made, because he usually got it right.

A close friend recalled Billy explaining how the Queen Mother found herself occasionally feeling a little depressed. On one of these days when nothing was planned and Billy could not find a way to enliven the day, he suggested the two of them take an impromptu lunch at the Ritz.

The Queen Mother was delighted at the idea and when they arrived she insisted they should not take a private room but should instead eat in the public dining room. The shock on the faces of the other diners was something Billy never forgot. They fell silent and the Queen Mother did her usual smile and wave. But it was a rather long luncheon and no one dared leave until at last the Queen Mother and Billy rose from their table. As she left, the other diners – no doubt intensely relieved their ordeal was over – broke into applause.

As he grew older Billy's taste for outrageous gossip increased.

'People who know nothing about William always say he was discreet and that that was why the royals were so devoted to him,' recalled Noel Kelly.

> That is a complete misunderstanding. They loved him for exactly the opposite reason – they loved him because he was so indiscreet, but in a confined way. He loved gossip and though he would never talk to the press or to someone who might talk to the press he nonetheless told his friends every juicy bit of gossip he could muster. Half the time I think he made it all up or at least exaggerated shamelessly for the sake of a good story. He loved to embellish. And he felt he could say whatever he liked about the Queen Mother and the other royals just so long as he was talking to someone he viewed as a trusted friend. But he took huge risks with his gossip as he did with his drinking and promiscuity and I'm amazed that more tales didn't leak to the press because he really did have a large number of friends and acquaintances. I think it is perhaps testimony to his instinctive ability to judge character that he didn't get into terribly hot water more often.

Billy also loved to explain how the old Queen made no allowances for the fact that he was getting on a bit.

'She insists on dancing with me at least once a day,' he would say. 'She's a very good dancer but she will insist that I sweep her off her feet!'

He tried always to emphasise the informality of his relationship with the Queen Mother. He liked people to think that she confided in him, which she certainly did, but he exaggerated the extent to which she did this. The truth was actually a curious mix of informality and strict, almost archaic formality.

Noel Kelly explains:

> There was a curious atmosphere among royal servants, an atmosphere that dated back to the days when royalty, the aristocracy and even the middle classes could afford dozens of servants. So the tradition of referring to servants by their first names was kept up – the Queen Mother always called Billy William – and some people thought this was an example of how the royal family had lost some of its old-fashioned stuffiness. In fact pages and other servants had always been referred to by their first names to emphasise their lowly status. No servant in Clarence House would have dared call Ralph Anstruther Ralph, or Alastair Aird Alastair, but they always used the lower servants' first names. It was a class thing dating back to Edwardian times and earlier when pages had been young boys.

DESPITE HAVING ONLY a few weeks to live and being in considerable pain, Reg insisted on donning his best white tie and tails on the morning of the Queen Mother's one hundredth birthday in 2000. He presented her with gifts from the domestic staff along with her usual cup of tea. The other servants were astonished to see him at all as he had been so ill. He could barely walk, in fact, as his leukaemia had been exacerbated by the return of a viral infection. A few hours after presenting that birthday cup of tea, Reg collapsed and was taken by ambulance to hospital where he was rushed into intensive care. He died a short while later.

Billy was distraught. The two men had been colleagues and lovers for nearly four decades and he confided to friends that Reg's death somehow felt like the beginning of the end. If Reg had gone, then the Queen Mother was not likely to be far behind.

Billy retreated to his little house on the Mall. And it was here that, for a time, he descended into drink. He once complained that for quite some time after Reg died he found it difficult to enjoy the pictures and photographs he had so carefully collected over the years. 'What is the point when there is no one else to enjoy them with me?' he said.

Billy had been at the Royal Opera House with the Queen Mother when news reached him that Reg had collapsed, and when he died a week later Billy began the meticulous process of organising an elaborate funeral for him at the Queen's Chapel in Marlborough Place.

A fellow servant at the time remembered stumbling into Billy's office sometime after Reg died and finding the elderly butler quietly weeping as he sorted his various papers. Unusually, Billy was not in the least put out by the intrusion. He simply said, 'I'm sorry, I'm rather upset at the moment. Would you mind coming back a little later?' It was typical of a man who could be vindictive at one moment, witty the next and finally quite open about his distress.

He told friends that he felt lost and rudderless, but his real anguish only came out when he drank and he was certainly drinking heavily at this time, partly because he was upset at losing Reg but also because his strength – and he was an immensely strong man – was beginning to ebb. It was not exactly that he was ill, although as one close friend put it 'he just wasn't right' after Reg died; it was as if some of the cords that bound him so tightly had weakened or snapped.

But Billy's ill health was also the result of decades spent drinking too much and working hideously long hours. There were rumours too that he had developed HIV. Other staff occasionally heard him crashing around while working late in his office but no one dared check on him. 'He would definitely fall asleep at his desk,' recalled one, 'and then sometimes wake in the early hours and carry on as if nothing had happened.'

> I once saw him asleep on the floor and I was told that he used to try
> to do exercises when he was drunk. He would try a few press-ups and
> then give up and go to sleep. He was once interrupted trying to do a
> cartwheel across the floor.

Billy's drinking became a serious matter in the last decade of the Queen Mother's life. On one occasion Sir Alastair Aird asked to see Billy on the pretext of discussing one of the junior footmen. He mentioned some minor misdemeanour and then in a manner that he clearly thought reasonable and diplomatic he gently mentioned that one or two people had been talking about Billy's drinking; they had said he seemed to be slightly the worse for wear by mid-afternoon each day. Billy was outraged and not just because he knew that the Queen Mother would always back him against Aird. On this occasion he adopted his usual tactic: he simply stood up, turned on his heel and walked out without a word. He slammed the door. Aird was furious but knew there was nothing he could do – for now. Reporting Billy to the Queen Mother would be worse than useless. There is no doubt that this was one of those occasions, and there were many, when Aird thought Billy should have been sacked or at least quietly retired. He is known to have confided in the other equerries that the Queen Mother was entirely unreasonable about Billy, who Aird felt was a dangerous liability.

In a remarkable echo of the John Brown–Queen Victoria romance, during which top level meetings were convened to discuss how to get rid of Brown, Aird got together with various other officials in a secret meeting to discuss the 'Tallon issue'. What exactly was agreed is not known but the meeting would at least have given these men (who were used to getting their own way) a chance to let off steam, and there is no doubt that meetings like this eventually paved the way for Billy's removal from Clarence House in the weeks following the death of the Queen Mother.

Those who knew Aird speak warmly of him. Major Colin Burgess, who was an equerry at Clarence House for a number of years, is on record as saying that Aird was a decent man, but Burgess – who was from a similar military background – would probably have shared Aird's views about the importance of the right tie and shoelaces. At times, Burgess's memoir makes Aird sound like a rather benign but fussy old nanny.

The fact that the Queen Mother always backed Billy when there was a row, proved, in the long run, to be a disaster. It meant he was safe only while she lived. A number of commentators have pointed out that Billy was so obsessed with the Queen Mother that he failed to see the wider picture or to consider the future – his own future. He must have known he would almost certainly outlive the Queen Mother, yet he enjoyed making enemies among those who, once she was dead, would suddenly have the power to get rid of him.

In a conversation a year or two after he retired to Kennington, Billy insisted that he had not deliberately twitted and teased the various equerries. He insisted it was simply that they did not understand the Queen Mother as he did, and as he always put her interests first it didn't bother him in the slightest if the equerries' noses were sometimes put out of joint. And he had some inkling that his position might become precarious.

He said:

I had served the Queen Mother in the same way for so long and according to the standards I thought she would expect so, as she moved towards the end of her life, I couldn't change just to ensure I had a softer landing after she died than might otherwise have been the case. Besides, the damage – if there was any – had already been done.

The equerries and various advisers and I had worked together for years, in some cases decades, and nothing I did in the last years of the Queen Mother's life was going to make any difference. If I had enemies, and I know I did, then they were always going to remember things that blackened my character. I'm not mentioning any names and I was certainly part of the intrigue and gossip at Clarence House, but however hard I might have tried it would always have been unlikely that I would be allowed to live on at Gate Lodge. I sort of knew it but thought I might be lucky – that I might just be left in peace if the Queen Mother left specific instructions that I should have Gate Lodge for as long as I liked. And I was told by the Queen Mother that she would instruct the household to that effect. She even said she would write a letter confirming it.

Even without enemies, Billy must have known it was going to be difficult because it has always been the case that when a member of the royal family dies all the relevant staff lose their jobs automatically. Press enquiries immediately following the death of the Queen Mother produced the following frosty response from a palace spokesman: 'When any member of the royal family dies their staff, in effect, become redundant.'

In terms of redundancy payments, the lower staff are paid so little that financial recompense is insignificant, while the equerries almost always have private incomes and are not paid anyway. Some of the servants who suddenly find themselves without a job are offered other jobs – often in the royal household – but this is by no means certain.

As the 1990s slowly passed Billy spent more weekends quietly in the Kennington flat he had once shared with Reg, but he still thought of Gate Lodge as home and he was convinced, despite his misgivings, that the Queen Mother's instructions about what should happen to him after her death would ensure that, at the very least, he could hope for a relatively soft landing.

For now there was work to do. If the Queen Mother had a less busy public schedule as she reached her mid-nineties she still loved to entertain at home, which meant that in many ways Billy was as busy as ever, despite his own increasingly poor health.

Billy still saw his friends regularly at his champagne parties. He still saw an occasional visitor from Coventry and still went out to pick up young men who were then slipped past the guards at Clarence House just as they had been in the old days, only now the policemen probably believed Billy when he said, 'Oh, he's just staying for tea.'

As the Queen Mother grew increasingly frail she continued to rely on Billy, but doctors and others became involved and as she weakened and became confused other advisers whom Billy had formerly been able to keep at bay were able to exert greater influence. She accepted the need for a younger team to nurse her, especially as her lunch and dinner parties came to an end. Billy knew he was being frozen out. He was convinced as he always had been that in matters relating to the Queen Mother's health he was the best judge of what was good for her, but by now his voice was increasingly drowned out by experts of one kind or another.

He was hurt by this because he had actually had a great deal of experience of looking after her when she was ill. He was always there when she went down with colds and occasional bouts of flu – she would insist that only Billy should be allowed to make what he described as a royal hot toddy. 'It was strong enough to numb all feeling!' he said later.

But more seriously he also helped when she had two hip operations and took some months to recover. He was one of the very few people she would allow to take her arm – so long as they were in private – and help steady her. And he was her main source of solace after a cataract operation. He later said she hated to be immobile and was by no means a good patient.

As Billy had less to do with the Queen Mother and she began seriously to decline, he saw a little more of the other royals, or at least those who had always liked him. Billy had always got on very well with Prince Charles and, alone among members of the immediate royals, he was to visit Billy in hospital a few months before he died.

Charles had written numerous letters to Billy when he was a child and Billy had always seemed wonderfully entertaining and avuncular to the young prince. Charles never forgot and when rumours reached him that, following the Queen Mother's death, Billy was struggling to survive on his tiny pension, the Prince is said to have added £100 a month.

The extent of Billy's gradual separation from the Queen Mother can be gathered from the fact that when she finally died in her sleep aged 101, Billy was not told the news by a member of the royal household. Whatever his faults, this might seem a particularly callous way to treat someone who had been so close to her for so long. It was no doubt the result of the equerries sensing that at last they had the upper hand. Billy's feeling that he had simply been cut adrift can be judged by a comment he made to his friend Basia Briggs on a number of occasions during the last few years of the Queen Mother's life. He said: 'I don't even know if she likes me anymore.'

Billy knew from newspaper and television reports that she was close to death but he was so shocked he could hardly speak when a reporter from a tabloid finally rang him to tell him the news. In the only interview Billy ever gave to the media – it is a thirty-second clip snatched as Billy tried to reach Gate Lodge soon after the Queen Mother died – he said simply, 'I loved her'.

Anyone who has seen the clip will detect something very slightly theatrical in Billy's words, but they are nonetheless charged with deep emotion and they express perfectly the sense one has that the Queen Mother was partly Billy's employer, partly a maternal figure and partly the central figure in his romantic world. He was in love with her as perhaps the medieval troubadours were in love with those unattainable French queens. The point of their adoration was that the object of it should be and remain ultimately unobtainable. Unlike Queen Victoria's servant John Brown, who, it is said, was rather bossy and even scolded her occasionally, Billy was genuinely besotted. For him, the Queen Mother could do no wrong, although she might be badly advised by others.

Billy certainly knew about her extravagance but he shared her view that a queen should not have to bother about money. He hated the suggestion that she was selfish and self-centred, an accusation that others have levelled at her. He was also certain that a vital piece of paper had been lodged in the right quarter to guarantee his future after her death. When he was pressed about this he always insisted that it was the household staff, jealous of his influence over the Queen Mother, who had deliberately destroyed this document in the days after her death.

> I think they knew that she would have been upset that I was simply made to leave Gate Lodge. The Queen Mother had promised that after my years of service it would be my home for life. I thought she had left instructions to that effect but I could hardly ask her to put it in writing to *me*. I suppose I was rather naïve in thinking that a letter would survive if it meant everyone had to put up with me for a few more years. In some ways they were quite ruthless, you know.

Though Billy hated to complain, he missed his earlier life terribly once the Queen Mother died. It was some months later that he received a short letter telling him that Gate Lodge had to be vacated. The deadline gave him little time to prepare, but obedient to the command he packed his things and left. There was no leaving party, no letter of thanks, no formal goodbye; an official made sure he was out on time and that all his things had been cleared ready for exile in south London.

THE BIGGEST PROBLEM now that life at Clarence House was over for Billy was that though he had numerous friends and acquaintances, he worried that many of them had enjoyed his company because of what he did rather than because of who he was. But, as it turned out, he need not have worried. His friends stuck by him and there were always new friends. But even Billy could not fill all his time with parties and his fifty-one years of service had given him no time to learn how to live in the evenings and at weekends when work is over and there are no parties to go to. For more than half a century Billy's work and life had been one and the same thing. Now he was on his own.

For years he had organised lunches and dinners for the Queen Mother, but he had never had to make his own meals or wash up – and these were tasks he hated. They made him realise that though he had been a servant, he had enjoyed a uniquely privileged life with dozens of staff at one time effectively working below him, awed by his presence.

'Oh, he loved it,' recalled one friend, 'because every day in the palace when he passed a junior footman, a gardener or a maid or even a lady in waiting he could tell they were looking across at him and thinking, "That's the legendary William Tallon!"'

> It was a curious sort of fame and localised power but nonetheless real for all that. And that is what he really missed when it was all over, which is not to say that he did not miss the Queen Mother too. He did, but if he had been allowed to stay in Gate Lodge after she died – as might easily have happened – he would have been happy and I think might have lived a little longer.

As it was, he shambled along to the shops and bought his food like any other elderly, retired, single man. But he was hopeless at it and began to eat irregularly and sometimes not at all. He was also shocked at the cost of a good bottle of wine as he hadn't had to buy wine himself for decades. He occasionally had to drink what he described as 'plonk' and even, at his worst moments, ate out of tins. He kept his sense of humour, though, remarking once, 'I suppose if beans were good enough for Anstruther they should be good enough for me.'

Billy had developed a taste for the finer things in life and he was suddenly cut off from them all. He found himself in what some people called a 'scruffy, run-down part of Kennington' shambling along the streets to the corner shop, with a plastic bag and his shirt tails hanging out.

But there were compensations. Because Billy was an amusing man with a remarkable employment history, he was invited to a seemingly endless series of parties which gave him a faint glow of the life he had once enjoyed with the Queen Mother. Occasionally he felt out of place at these gatherings, but then he often under-valued his own virtues as an entertaining and witty dinner guest. As another friend recalled:

> Billy sometimes went into terrible glooms that were alleviated only by alcohol. He drank, I think, because he really was an alcoholic in the sense that he relied on alcohol; he relied on having it every day but it was a habit he had got into at Clarence House over many years and he found that even though he couldn't afford the sort of things he was used to, he had to have something – alcohol restored some of his charm, his confidence and his wit. But the fact that he was no longer

drinking the finest wines in the finest company – as he saw it – took a lot of getting used to and he never really managed it.

He went to parties in Chelsea and Belgravia, in Highgate and Kensington and he was treated in a way that other ordinary ex-servants would never have been treated. He was the grand old man of royal service. It was his unique status, his numerous appearances – admittedly in the background – at royal events, his medals [which included the very rarely awarded Royal Victorian Gold Medal for long service] that made him special. It was all these things that made him a celebrity. And the great thing about Billy was that in his exile he became a humbler figure, some might even say a nicer man. Power had corrupted him a little and he knew it. He had been beastly, he once said, to some of those who worked for him and I think he felt rather bad about it.

Everyone speculated about whether he was writing his memoirs and a number of his friends were absolutely convinced that by the time he died he had written a very great deal.

Another close friend of Billy's said:

He was definitely writing something, which is perhaps why so many odd things happened after he died. I'm sure that in the same way that someone probably destroyed the Queen Mother's instructions that Billy should be allowed to stay on at Gate Lodge, they also destroyed whatever it was he had written about his life with the Queen Mother at Clarence House. Why else would a team of people have arrived at the Kennington flat to go through his things so soon after he died? They were there for several days and a great many of Billy's things vanished as a result.

But if Billy had written about his life in service he did not talk about it much among his friends.

'I heard people at parties try to draw him out but it never worked,' recalled a journalist and television scriptwriter who knew Billy in his last years.

> This was partly the habit of a lifetime, I think, but partly also that whatever the tabloids might like to think, Billy wanted to save his best stories for publication. The royals, as he explained to me on a number of occasions, grow up in such an exposed way – exposed to public scrutiny – that they are very careful about what they say and do, but they still have lives to lead with all the mistakes and confusions that can involve. And Billy had known them all for so long. He knew the scandals and the tittle-tattle.
>
> Billy had seen the Queen Mother tipsy on many occasions and he'd seen her lose her temper or do absurd things, but his main aim in writing his memoirs would not have been to show her in a bad light. It would have concentrated on the eccentrics who run Clarence House and might well have been Billy's revenge on the equerries who he felt had treated him so badly.
>
> He certainly also knew a great deal. He knew for example, or at least said he knew, that Princess Diana was having affairs while still married to Prince Charles and long before it was generally known that the marriage was in trouble. He also knew a great deal about the younger generation of royals.

Billy admired earlier monarchs who had remained loyal to their spouses even if they had also enjoyed the favours of numerous mistresses. He thought it unseemly for members of the royal family to get divorced and felt that in this respect the Queen Mother's grandchildren had somehow let the side down. He felt the role of the royals was to provide the majesty, the ceremony and the spectacle that gave so many people so much pleasure. Ironically, given his own decline, he was hugely scathing about the younger royals drinking too much and tumbling out of clubs at two o' clock in the morning.

Billy survived the death of his employer for five years, which was much longer than many of his friends expected. Despite his banishment – and he saw it as banishment rather than that he had simply been made redundant – he retained an inner strength which he himself claimed came from his mother. It was this strength that enabled him to cope with the last and in some ways most difficult period of his life, a period made far worse by the behaviour of a ruthless group of tabloid journalists and photographers.

Chapter Sixteen

Twilight

OR THE WHOLE of the last five years of his life Billy was pursued, sometimes night and day, by photographers who pushed their cameras into his face and by journalists who walked alongside him, sometimes for miles, asking a continual stream of questions, none of which Billy ever answered. Some journalists tried to break into his house while others found out where he was going in the evening and bribed other dinner guests to get him drunk while they waited outside hoping he would say something indiscreet or fall over.

When continual pestering failed, some of the journalists began phoning Billy and pretending to be one or other of his friends; others tried to photograph him through the windows of his flat, especially early in the morning or late at night, hoping they might catch a picture of him half-dressed. Journalists were frequently seen digging through his dustbins, but Billy fought back as best he could.

> I put cat shit in my bin some days and smear it on a few typed sheets of paper on which I've written a few bits of gibberish and slightly torn, and it's wonderful to see how gleefully they pick it all out and get very excited in case they may have discovered something really interesting.

On one occasion Billy confessed he had urinated in a plastic bag which he had filled with old letters and bills that were of absolutely no use to anyone.

'Oh, it was wonderful to see how excited they were about that,' he said.

> It gave me a wonderful laugh. It was like a tonic, but that's all you can do. You have to fight them in any way you can. Ringing the police doesn't help a bit because pestering someone night and day is perfectly legal so long as you can say you are a journalist. I could understand it if I'd committed a terrible crime or something but I haven't so why don't they leave me alone?

One journalist who had been among those pursuing Billy at this time recalled the pressure he and his colleagues were under.

> Everyone was convinced that if Billy told his story it would be absolutely sensational. The important thing was not what Billy might have said but what he would put his name to – we tried everything from sending very pretty boys around to knock on the door and chat him up, to older women journalists we thought might remind him of the old Queen Mother, but nothing worked. We even tried offering him a lot of money, but he wasn't biting. Some us began to admire him after a while because he almost never lost his temper and if it had been me I think I might have punched someone!

Billy knew that assaulting a journalist would have been a disaster because it was exactly what they wanted. Once they knew he wouldn't give them a story about his years with the Queen Mother, the only other option was to provoke him into doing something outrageous.

His lowest point came in October 2002 when he was returning from a party to launch a book by interior designer Nicky Haslam. Someone had promised to take Billy home but a last-minute muddle meant he returned to Kennington alone. Already drunk, he foolishly stopped at the Dog House and continued drinking. When he tried to get home he fell and was photographed sprawled in the gutter.

Meanwhile the partying continued. Billy was determined not to become reclusive in the face of the press onslaught. But his taste for partying wasn't quite what it had once been.

'I think I go to these things sometimes because I find it so difficult to be on my own,' he confessed.

> I'm just not used to it and I'm too old to get used to it now. I'd rather
> sit in the pub because at least there is someone to talk to there. I enjoy
> some of the parties of course, but would happily give them up if I
> could go back to my old life.

For many of his friends it was a shock to see Billy in his old, beautifully cut dark suit or in bizarrely ill-matched shirt and trousers wandering rather shakily to the corner shop to buy a cheap bottle of wine. Or, more dangerously, he would spend night after night in the Dog House. He would get drunk and invite absolutely anyone – and everyone – back to the flat. His friends worried he would be beaten up or have his things stolen. But, for Billy, anything was better than sitting in the flat alone.

Getting through the day was even more difficult because he hated cooking for himself and, as we have seen, despised washing up. However, despite this reluctance to spend any time in the kitchen, a number of his friends recall that when he could be bothered he was rather a good cook. 'He only really enjoyed it if he was cooking for others – for those friends who came to see him.'

He could not afford a cleaner or home help and the flat's kitchen occasionally became a mess. He admitted that he tended to sit and brood during the day but loved it when old friends called and he was always delighted to be asked to lunch.

One of the royals who always remained on good terms with Billy was Lord Snowdon. The two had known each other for decades.

But if Lord Snowdon was sympathetic to Billy's plight, he perhaps failed to understand the key issue: Billy felt he had been a part of the royal family rather than simply employed by them. He had learned to live in many ways as the royals lived, with servants to buy and cook his food and wash his clothes. It was as difficult for Billy to live an ordinary life as it would have been for anyone so completely institutionalised. Everyone knew that what Billy really needed – and many would argue deserved – was a grace-and-favour apartment.

Snowdon did his best, however, and when a journalist wrote a long, slightly malicious feature about how the two men met regularly every week for lunch – something that they had not in fact done until then – Snowdon was so incensed that he immediately rang Billy and arranged that they should indeed meet for lunch. It was an attempt to beat the journalists at their own game.

'That's the only favour the press ever did me!' Billy would comment wryly. He loved these lunches and in many ways they helped fill the enormous gap left in his life.

Any contact with the family for whom he had worked so long was welcome, as was contact with old friends who remained in service. One or two of the junior staff with whom he had got on well came to see him. One recalled:

Billy was nothing but kindness to me and I can assure you there were no sexual advances at all. I only worked at Clarence House for a few years but my memories of Billy are all of his kindness and his humour. I went to see him twice in Kennington after he retired and he made a special effort with tea and cakes, and I noticed the tea was expensive and the cake very good. But somehow the flat didn't look as Gate Lodge had looked. The lodge seemed to reflect someone who loved his life and was proud of what he had achieved. The pictures were all carefully hung and the photos carefully displayed, but in the Kennington flat there was a slightly gloomy, disordered air and the pictures and other items sometimes looked as if they had lost their sparkle. In that way I think they reflected the fact that Billy himself had lost interest in life to some extent.

The last time I saw Billy he had just returned from shopping and he was decidedly unsteady on his feet. His hair had lost its lustre and it was rather wispy, though he still kept it fairly long. There was a lot more grey in it than I'd ever seen before. The thing that really shocked me was his red face and sagging jowls. His once bright eyes had also dimmed and they had the classic yellowy-red look of the heavy drinker. His suit was in a bit of a mess too, at least compared to how it looked in happier days, but I knew that this was all because he was unhappy and struggled to look after himself.

But if some of Billy's friends recalled his unhappiness, others tell a different story. Caroline Butler, whose family lived near Billy's flat in Kennington, remembered a more resilient character. Like many of his friends she felt that Billy had been rather let down by the royal household, but she remembered that he was still capable of enjoying himself despite his loss. She recalled watching the film *The Queen* with him and his reaction to it. He thought it was accurate, except that it showed the Queen Mother having breakfast with other members of the family. He insisted she always had breakfast in bed.

Caroline Butler believes Billy was reasonably happy in his Kennington retirement. She points out that tabloid stories about a run-down council estate in south London were entirely wrong and that the flat in Chester Way was in an attractive area. She also insisted Billy's flat was bright and clean and beautifully decked out with all the things he and Reg had collected over the years.

She recalled the street lined with flowering cherry trees, and remembered how, in earlier years, Billy and Reg had proudly showed off their works of art, which included sketches of Princess Margaret and Princess Elizabeth by the designer Norman Hartnell. According to Caroline, Billy's proudest possession was a photograph of Reg with the Queen Mother at his side and taken on the Kennington flat's patio.

WHATEVER LIFE BILLY was able to carve out for himself in Kennington it was still a far cry from Gate Lodge. Caroline Butler's memories of Billy in his final years are surprisingly happy ones. She recalled him being in her parents' flat often or dining at the Wolseley restaurant in Piccadilly. She confirms Lord Snowdon's regular visits, and insists that though he was occasionally prone to melancholy Billy was generally happy.

But other friends were not so sanguine; they noticed only Billy's desperation for company, his dislike of being alone and his palpable air of simply not being able to cope with the mundane tasks of everyday life.

As another friend said, 'He could cope with gaiety and fun, with partying and dining out – especially at his local Italian restaurant, Amici, which he loved – but when he woke in the morning alone and with not much to do each day he despaired.'

He was not entirely abandoned, however. Prince Charles, in addition to generously boosting Billy's pension, invited him to tea at Clarence House on several occasions during the last months of his life and Billy returned the compliment by inviting Charles down to Kennington, where tea was served in the beautiful cups that the Queen Mother had given Billy all those years ago.

CONVERSATIONS WITH BILLY during what he sometimes called his 'exile' revealed a man who wanted to unburden himself but found it difficult. He paid tribute to his Kennington neighbours who tried their best to make life easier for him by inviting him to parties and lunches.

However unhappy he felt at any particular time, he refused to hear a word against the Queen Mother, but it always seemed that there was something slightly odd – something almost pathological about this. 'It wasn't entirely rational,' as one of his Kennington neighbours said.

We all knew she must have been difficult at times and no one would have thought he was being disloyal if he'd grumbled about her now and then. The fact is he had to have an absolutely fixed point in his life and it was her.

He just kept saying, 'I loved her, you know', and tears would well up in his eyes. He reserved his anger for the royal household and though his sense of being hard done by increased in the years after he left royal service, I think he was perfectly rational and in many ways perhaps not nearly as angry as he might have been in the circumstances. He was particularly cross with Anstruther and Aird, the former equerries who he accused of working behind his back and showing a complete lack of respect for the Queen Mother's wishes. He was really quite bitter about it all.

But it was certainly not all doom and gloom. A friend who saw him frequently in his last year or two said, 'He loved to talk about the happy times, especially in the distant past. He would begin to talk quietly about all the fun he had during his years of service.

"'Do you know," he would say, "we often danced together when no one else was around."

'She used to tell me she had enjoyed dancing as a girl but now only rarely had the chance. She felt it would be seen as rather undignified except privately at the annual gillies' ball at Balmoral, but she would often get up and ask me to take a few steps with her, which I rather enjoyed. She also told me the equerries were always trying to get her to do things she didn't want to do. "Including get rid of you, William!" she would say.

'I think she was teasing slightly but then she was a terrific tease. One very curious thing about her was that I can never remember her fully losing her temper with anyone.

'It was all part of her wonderful self-control, something the royal family in general are so good at. Losing one's temper is definitely seen as very unseemly but she had something far more important than temper. She had an extraordinary ability with just a slight change in her look and her bearing to bring you to heel. I think I was rather in love with this power she had and it's a power HM the Queen has too, but not the younger generation.'

Billy loved the fact that the Queen Mother, though rarely indiscreet herself, loved to hear others gossiping, especially if the gossip concerned famous people she had met and especially if they were gay. She particularly loved stories about Sir John Gielgud and his legendary forgetfulness. 'We arranged to meet many times for lunch,' she quipped, 'and he did occasionally remember.'

Noël Coward stories were also a favourite. She herself had once accompanied Coward to the theatre and on seeing him glancing at a row of guardsmen lined up to greet her, she said, 'Oh Noël, do be careful; they count them when they put them out, you know.'

She loved to tease Billy, too. When unfavourable stories about one of her distant relatives appeared in the papers, she said to Billy, 'Well, we all have skeletons in our cupboards, don't we, William?'

She then paused and added, 'And some of our cupboards have to be rather large, do they not?'

She kept her sense of humour to the end and in the last months before failing health prevented her from seeing Billy, she said to him rather poignantly, as if aware that the end could not be that far off, 'We're two old dears, really, aren't we, William? But we've had some fun.'

Billy admitted that in the last fifteen years of her life she had become increasingly dotty, 'but in such a charming way', and he rather enjoyed being able to come to the rescue, as it were, more often.

He loved to repeat the story of how she almost 'came unstuck' once while driving along the Mall.

Yes, that was a little awkward. We were being driven slowly along the Mall in one of the big official cars and she was doing her wonderful graceful smile with her head tilted to one side and waving steadily at the crowds along the route. She'd had a few gins that morning, but no more than usual – and I know that because I poured them myself – so everything should have been fine. Then, out of the corner of my eye I noticed that, very slowly, she was sliding off the slippery leather seat at the back of the car and down on to the floor. As she sank out of sight she continued to smile and wave as if oblivious to the fact that the crowds could no longer see her. She just carried on smiling and waving until she was hauled back up into position – by me. And then she carried on as if nothing had happened. She was so absolutely devoted to duty that that was typical of her. Sometimes, of course, she got confused and I saw her once in Clarence House waving regally when only the corgis were around.

Billy's reluctance to tell more negative stories in later life was entirely superficial. It depended on who he was with and in his last years he was definitely more open than he had been in earlier days.

It's very difficult to get a flavour of his conversation, but the following gives a good example of how entertaining – and almost indiscreet – he could be:

> Before lunch the Queen Mother would always say, 'I do hope lunch is late, then we can have another drink or perhaps several. Won't that be fun?'
>
> And the conversations at lunch *could* be huge fun, although the footmen had to try to keep straight faces. The royals in the 1960s and 1970s were probably the only family in England who still had footmen waiting at table.
>
> I remember, at a lunch for one of the Queen Mother's favourite charities, she was talking about the animal rights movement, of which she certainly did not approve at all. She explained that she had to keep all her fur coats locked up: 'One has to be careful, you see – they might pour paint over one.'
>
> 'Or set fire to one,' quipped Princess Margaret, who was sitting next to the Queen Mother. They then both fell about in fits of giggles.
>
> At the same lunch the conversation turned to Prince Philip and someone mentioned the fact that he liked poetry.
>
> 'How extraordinary,' said the Queen Mother. 'I have known Philip

all these years yet I did not know he had a guilty secret. He likes poetry. Poor man. How dreadful.'

The Queen Mother loved television and she did several very good imitations of well-known comic characters. Her Blackadder was very good, but best of all was her extraordinary attempt to imitate the comedian Ali G.

So she would say, 'Darling, lunch was simply marvellous – respec'.'

She loved to tease and she teased all the members of her family as well as me. When she visited Prince William at the University of St Andrews she would ask him repeatedly to make a date so that she could come and spend the night in his room in college. Every summer she would begin to drop hints that she would like to spend a week at Kennington and did I know anywhere suitable. She would say, 'And do you think when I come to Kennington you would be able to organise a few parties? Then we can forget all our troubles and be gay for a while.'

Often after lunch or dinner she would get up and do a few comic dance steps that looked rather like a Billy Dainty routine – I'm sure it was based on his antics because she loved watching him on television.

Billy often reminded his friends that several of the Queen Mother's cousins had spent their whole lives in lunatic asylums. He would quip that she herself could seem slightly mad, or at least eccentric. And this eccentricity showed itself in other ways.

One of her closest friends, a former lady in waiting, said the Queen Mother had almost no idea how to dress herself and had the aristocratic idea that it was appalling to have to know whether one's slip went on before one's skirt.

'I always had to remind her to go to the lavatory before we left for any kind of event,' she recalled, 'and on several occasions she locked herself in. A dainty little voice would be heard saying, "Terribly difficult to open this door. Could anyone help?" Eventually I waited discreetly outside and later suggested she leave it unlocked in future.'

At lunch with friends or at dinner in Amici's, Billy would happily tell these and other of his favourite stories about his former employer – just so long as no journalists were present.

He said she had a sharp tongue and a rich and slightly eccentric turn of phrase when she chose to.

There often seemed something very funny about the gap between what she said and her beautiful, upper-class accent. But she didn't give a fig what anyone thought of her or what she said so long as she wasn't written about in the wrong way in the newspapers.

But when she decided to let off a bit of steam, it was a shock for many of the servants who, like me, grew up thinking members of the royal family were saints.

Many of the maids who worked at Balmoral, for example, were from small Presbyterian villages in remote areas of Scotland. They'd grown up in communities where the children's swings were padlocked on Sundays and where laughing was considered sinful if it meant people could see your teeth! They hardly knew what swearing was! The royal family liked their servants to be from these remote areas because they thought they would be serious, quiet and biddable.

I remember one of the maids telling me she always put cotton wool in her ears in case she heard any cursing from the Queen Mother, which I found hard to believe because I don't think the Queen Mother ever swore. Another maid explained that she didn't mind when the Queen Mother threw things at her because ten minutes later the old lady would tilt her head and smile as if nothing had happened. She was cantankerous one minute and all smiles the next.

She was also famous for her practical jokes and when an official she had not met before came to Balmoral for the first time she might shake hands with him and say, 'I'm so glad you have come to look at the boiler. It has been playing up for some time.' I think she enjoyed the look of utter confusion on their faces. One or two of the more malicious servants would claim that she really did think they had come to fix the boiler or unblock a sink, but I absolutely refute this!

Chapter Seventeen

Farewell

B Y EARLY 2007, Billy looked increasingly vulnerable and throughout that year his health deteriorated rapidly. He'd been visited in March by Prince Charles after a spell in St Mary's Hospital in Paddington and Prince Charles was apparently shocked at his old friend's decline. Billy's conversation and behaviour became increasingly erratic and confused in the last months of his life, yet the royal household, which must have been aware of what was going on, seems to have done little to help him. It could be argued of course that he had long ceased to be employed by the Palace and therefore it was not for them to keep tabs on him. If that is true – and of course it would certainly be true of any other employer – then what happened immediately after Billy's death is all the more strange. As we will see, as soon as Billy died, officials gained entry to his flat and spent several days going through his things.

In the meantime, Billy's last few months were a mixture of odd flashes of the old Billy – in the evenings when he was invited to parties – and gloomy days spent filling time. On one occasion he was spotted by a neighbour in the local launderette desperately trying to find coins to operate the machine.

'He dropped his change all over the floor and I found him scrabbling on his knees and almost in tears,' recalled the neighbour. On another occasion he was seen staggering back to the flat at eleven in the morning looking dishevelled and confused. He stopped and leaned against a lamppost every hundred yards or so as if he needed to catch his breath.

In the last year of his life Billy also began to speak far more often of his sadness at the way the royal household had treated him. He was so upset that he even talked about moving to France. His idea was to escape familiar scenes that were filled now with bitter memories, but also to escape the tabloid journalists who were still hounding him and trying to get him drunk in the hope that he would disgrace himself in some way. But, without selling his treasured possessions – his last mementoes of the Queen

Mother – such a move would have been impossible. 'I'm trapped,' he used to say. 'I have nothing to live for since she died but I don't seem to be able to die myself. It's terrible.'

In his bitterest moments he recalled how in the Queen Mother's last months he had asked if he could see her – he had been largely side-lined by this time – and permission was refused. The Queen Mother herself was by this time too confused to know what was happening around her. Weakened by extreme old age she was attended only by her medical staff and by the advisers who could now ignore Billy. Frustrated by repeated refusals to let him see his old employer, he at one point became hysterical and was told that if he did not calm down the police would be called.

'I was upset and they didn't care,' he told a friend.

> I thought they would have taken account of my long years with the Queen Mother. But as far as the household was concerned, I was simply an ex-employee. I can see why they would have viewed it in that way, but it did rather hurt. It was as if I'd worked in the palace for six months washing bottles and hardly been noticed by anyone. The truth is some members of the royal household rather enjoyed my unhappiness. It was time for their revenge. They knew the Queen Mother could no longer protect me so the knives were out. I suppose I was silly not to have known it would happen.

What Billy had not fully realised was that in a fundamental way Clarence House was like a medieval royal court and that royal favourites rarely survived the death of their protectors.

I was naïve, I suppose. The household disliked me because I was too close to the Queen Mother. I know that was their view because every now and then one of them would get angry with me and say it. I remember one of the advisers saying, 'Who on earth do you think you are?' He was furious because I had told him that Her Majesty the Queen Mother had insisted I stay close to her at a particular event. I replied, 'I'm a shopkeeper's son from Coventry but I'm afraid my company is preferable to yours.' I suppose it was silly of me to rise to the bait but I couldn't help it. The adviser went red in the face and stalked off. I'm afraid I enjoyed my little victory very much but I can't imagine he ever forgave me.

But Billy's troubles were to end far sooner than anyone could have expected. On 23 November 2007, he was found dead in his flat by a neighbour. The official cause of death was cardiac arrest – a heart attack – but Billy had been treated at an HIV clinic a few years earlier. His death was undoubtedly also brought on by years of heavy drinking, although he had no sense that the end was near. As one friend said, 'He did not expect to die that night. He had planned various lunches and parties over the ensuing days and he had a new interest – he was definitely writing down his memories of life at Clarence House.'

At the time of his death he was reported to be seriously underweight and friends said he had been drinking but not eating properly for years. However, the same friends had also noticed that his mood had lifted in his last weeks as he began to enjoy the process of writing about his life.

For the royal household, Billy was easier to deal with in death than he had been in life. The palace clearly felt that it would be too obvious a snub and cause public outrage if Billy were denied a funeral that reflected his lengthy devotion to the Queen Mother, so they made no attempt to prevent the funeral taking place in St James's Palace, an honour promised to Billy by the Queen Mother many years earlier. Tactically, of course, it was a shrewd move. The royal household would have hoped that rumours about their difficult relationship with Billy would be scotched if it was seen that he was given a splendid send-off.

You have to be rather special to expect your funeral to be held at the Queen's Chapel at St James's Palace. Originally the 'chapels royal' referred to a select group of singers and church officials who were permanently on hand to serve the spiritual needs of the monarch; it was only gradually that the phrase came to mean actual buildings. Today the term refers to two buildings – the Chapel Royal and the Queen's Chapel at St James's Palace.

St James's Palace itself is one of the oldest palaces still in use in the country and for various eccentric reasons, despite not having been lived in by a monarch for more than two centuries, it is still, officially, the residence of the sovereign. Ambassadors are all still accredited to the Court of St James's.

Much of St James's Palace has been re-modelled and re-built

over the centuries but the Queen's Chapel is largely unspoiled: it remains substantially as it was when built by the first great English classical architect, Inigo Jones. It was completed in 1625.

And it was here on 6 December 2007 that William Tallon, Page of the Backstairs and royal servant for almost fifty-two years, was remembered.

In addition to Lord Snowdon and his daughter Lady Sarah Chatto, guests included Sir Roy Strong, actors Patricia Routledge and June Brown, painters Roy Petley and Richard Stone and TV comic Paul O'Grady. The 200 guests had been chosen from more than 2,000 applications for tickets. One of Billy's very few surviving close relatives, his cousin Naomi, was also present.

Sir Derek Jacobi read the poem 'Words in Praise of Billy' by actor Leonard Whiting. The music, chosen by Billy himself, included the traditional (Mozart's 'Ave Verum') and the contemporary ('Mishima' by the American minimalist composer Philip Glass). The Reverend Prebendary William Scott described Billy's extraordinary loyalty to the Queen Mother, and the assembled guests sang 'Parry's Anthem', one of Billy's favourites. The service concluded with a reading of Billy's favourite song, 'Send In the Clowns', and then Billy's flower-strewn coffin left the chapel to the strains of Strauss's 'Radetzky March'.

No member of the immediate royal family was there. Even Prince Charles was busy elsewhere. His absence and that of other members of the immediate family was felt by some of Billy's closest friends to reflect the royals' ambivalent attitude to a man who, in their eyes, had, despite his great loyalty, over-stepped the mark; a man who had been too close to someone he was meant only to serve.

Soon after Billy's death, a small group of men were seen entering his Kennington flat. Within days, all Billy's possessions were boxed and in storage. There is no proof that things went missing, but the speed with which events occurred shocked Billy's friends, one of whom said:

> It was all very odd. Imagine if you had ceased to work for someone in 2003 and then five years later you die. Would you expect your former employer to visit your house and go through your things? That's what happened to Billy. We were sure the royal household had sent a team to go through Billy's possessions before they were sold.
>
> The material that came up for auction some time later represented just a small part of everything he had at the time of his death. I know that because I visited the flat regularly. Another oddity is that not a scrap of written material survived the visit by the unidentified team. I don't see how you could argue that they were just helping out by clearing the flat.
>
> And does anyone really believe that if they had found Billy's notebooks they would have preserved them? This seems highly unlikely even if you do not subscribe to some of the more extreme theories about Billy's death and what happened afterwards. By that, I mean some of the theories that he was bumped off. I don't think any of his friends really believe that, but it was all very odd.

Other neighbours were convinced that Billy had intended to leave little gifts to his many friends as he had no close family, yet these gifts did not materialise.

A close friend explains that Billy was terrified the royal household would accuse him of stealing his treasures, much as Paul Burrell, the late Princess of Wales's butler, was accused of theft after Diana's death. But Billy had taken precautions. On leaving Gate Lodge he had asked a lawyer to draw up a list of gifts he was taking to make sure that everything was signed for – that he had taken nothing, in other words, without permission.

Some months after the funeral, and with little warning, Billy's possessions came up for auction. His solicitor, who was also his executor, had made the decision to sell because, unknown to many of his friends, Billy had wanted the bulk of his estate, presumably minus those little gifts that had so mysteriously failed to materialise, to be sold to raise money for a leukaemia research charity. (Leukaemia had killed Reg Wilcox so the bequest was a fitting one.) News spread quickly and the sale aroused huge interest across the world. Curiously, a provincial auctioneer – James Grinter, of Reeman Dansie in Colchester, Essex – was chosen to conduct the sale. Many thought it would have raised a great deal more money if it had been conducted by one of the big London auctioneers, but the executor clearly felt that a few letters and mementos were unlikely to justify any great expectations. How wrong he was. It took more than ten hours to dispose of more than 700 lots.

The highlight of the sale was a short letter written by the Queen Mother to Billy asking him to make sure he had packed enough gin and Dubonnet for a trip to Scotland. The hand-written letter, which sparked a telephone bidding war, asks Billy to prepare for an outdoor lunch and finishes: 'I think that I will take two small bottles of Dubonnet and gin with me this morning, in case it is needed.' The letter's appeal came undoubtedly from its rarity – few letters written by the Queen Mother have ever come up for auction – but also from its light-hearted confirmation of the Queen Mother's fondness for gin. The letter went to an anonymous bidder for an astonishing £16,000.

The sale was expected to raise around £200,000 in total but such was the level of interest that the final sum was closer to half a million pounds.

Other highlights of the sale included a letter to Billy from Princess Diana. It was sent soon after the birth of Prince William and read simply: 'We are not sure at the moment what has hit us, except a very strong pair of lungs.'

The letter made £5,000. Seven other letters from the late Princess made a combined total of £15,000.

A portrait of the Queen Mother, a miniature version of a painting owned by the royal family, went for £30,000.

Despite the success of the sale, still rumours lingered that much of Billy's material had gone missing, especially his black book, as his diary was known, and those memoirs he was thought to be writing at the time of his death.

But the assumption that these memoirs might have been especially revealing, vindictive or damaging to the royal family may be entirely wrong. Billy may well have confined his recollections to his happier experiences. Certainly the dominant impression everyone took from even the briefest conversation with Billy was that he felt uniquely privileged to have worked for so long in a job that he loved as much as he loved anything else in his life. In lighter moments he confessed that any disagreements he may have had with his colleagues over the years were no more than one might expect in an environment where people from many different backgrounds worked closely together in sometimes difficult circumstances and for long hours.

'We were a family,' he would say, 'and all families squabble occasionally. In the grand scheme of things it doesn't mean anything.'

Certainly when he looked back on his long years of service he would have recalled the extraordinary gulf between that small boy in Coventry and the rather grand figure he was to become; a figure who could occasionally step out boldly into the Mall and expect all the traffic to come to a stop. Billy also had the consolation that from his earliest days he had always known what he wanted to do; whatever the difficulties and set-backs of later years he had never questioned his decision to work for an institution he loved unquestioningly. And at some deep level he probably knew that his overwhelming admiration for the Queen Mother and the royal family in general had sometimes blinded him to the sensitivities of others; he once said he knew he had over-stepped the mark on many occasions. He felt he always knew best but on looking back must have realised that his absolute self-belief and the arrogance it inspired could lead only to disappointment and regret.

But perhaps Billy, more than anyone, should have heeded the advice given to him by the Queen Mother herself. She understood the complexities of life at court perhaps better than anyone and almost at the beginning of their relationship she had said:

'Whatever you do, William, never trust anyone. *Ever.*'

Acknowledgements

THANKS TO EVERYONE who helped with the research for this book, but especially to Basia Briggs; and to Katy Quinn-Guest who took time off from a punishing schedule to read through an early draft and suggested numerous improvements. I also owe a debt of gratitude to Victoria Godden, my editor at the Robson Press, for patiently unravelling countless obscurities, and to Charlotte Wadham for high days and holidays.

Not in Front of the Corgis

SECRETS OF LIFE BEHIND
THE ROYAL CURTAINS

BRIAN HOEY

224PP PAPERBACK, £8.99

The Windsors are England's most famous family, but what are they really like when they're out of the public gaze?

Behind closed doors in every royal residence, from Buckingham Palace to Clarence House, there are two families – one upstairs and one down – and nobody knows a royal quite like a royal servant, intimately acquainted as they are with every quirk, foible and eccentricity.

This is the inside story of the royal family through the eyes of those who know them best, a sneak peek behind the ermine-trimmed curtains to reveal what they really get up to in their spare time. Are they just like us? Or are they are a world apart? Here are the answers to everything we've ever wondered about the royals: which programmes does the Queen watch on T.V? What is it like to attend a dinner party thrown by Charles and Camilla? Who are the most popular (and most unpopular!) royals to work for and why?

Not in Front of the Corgis is the real *Upstairs Downstairs* – a unique and fascinating collection of all the secrets you ever wanted to know about the royal family.

— AVAILABLE FROM ALL GOOD BOOKSHOPS —